MW01714912

SHAPE UP

The New Unisex Bodybuilding

SHAPE UP
THE NEW UNISEX BODYBUILDING

Robert Kennedy, A.T.D.

Illustrated

Jacket design by Steve and Ellen Davis of Steve Davis Fitness Center, Newhall, California

Fell's Books Fill Your Needs

Frederick Fell Publishers, Inc., New York

ISBN #0-8119-0300-1

Copyright © 1978, by Robert Kennedy

All rights reserved. No part of this work covered by the copyright herein may be reproduced or used in any form or by any means—graphic, electronic, or mechanical, including photocopying, recording, taping, or information storage and retrieval systems—without permission of the publisher.

For information address:

Frederick Fell Publishers, Inc.
386 Park Avenue South
New York, NY 10016

Published simultaneously in Canada by:
Thomas Nelson & Sons, Limited
Don Mills, Ontario, Canada

MANUFACTURED IN THE UNITED STATES OF AMERICA

1 2 3 4 5 6 7 8 9 0

Designed by Michael U. Polvere

CONTENTS

INTRODUCTION

The body you have now is your house. It is the home you were born with, and the home you will die with. Many people look after their cars far better than their bodies; cleaning, polishing, and dusting. Nothing is too much work. Yet, the truth is that they can trade that car in for a brand-new model almost anytime they like. You cannot do this with your body.

How can we justify giving a car the best gas and oil while feeding ourselves junk? What prompts you to run your car regularly, yet at the same time neglect to exercise your own body?

It's a weird truth—but nevertheless fact; Most of us treat our bodies with less respect than a car, bicycle. . .or even the kitchen stove.

Few people realize that most bodies can be completely reshaped. And most *need* reshaping.

Whether they recognize the fact or not, most men and women have figure problems. That is to say that their physical development is lacking in some way.

No one is perfect, and no one will ever be perfect in physical appearance, but we can all improve ourselves dramatically within the spectrum of our individual physical potential. In fact, it is this author's belief that with dedication and perseverance, *every* man and woman in normal health can improve his or her physical appearance to the extent that most observers would regard them as being physically perfect!

A qualified physical culture authority might be able to

find a few "flaws," but the average person would regard our subject as being in great shape.

So please understand that unless you are in poor health or "over the hill" chronologically, or by some quirk of nature have inherited irregular characteristics of some type, you can correct your figure problems. You can shape up your legs, lose fat from your hips and waist, improve your poise, firm up your limbs and become more sexy looking and generally far more attractive.

This book shows you how—and what's more it's not necessarily going to be a *gruelling* fight. Remember, a good habit is as easy to form as a bad habit. Simply follow the steps as outlined in this book. . .and progress will come. A new dynamic 'knockout' bodyshape can be yours. It's up to you!

PART I

LEARNING YOUR BODY

Steve Reeves, former Mr. America, Mr. World, Mr. Universe, seen here in a still from one of his box office record breaking 'Hercules' films, is an example of what sensible weight training can accomplish. Even today at past the half century mark Reeves has a body that few men half his age possess. In the physical culture world he is still regarded as 'Mr. Proportion,' having identical calf, upper arm and neck measurements, with the rest of his body in perfect balance.

Chapter I

BODYSHAPE—WHO NEEDS IT?

Just about everyone, at one time or another, decides to do something about their body. It may be that you suddenly get the "bug" to be fit and healthy, or else you may decide that you can't stand another day of being overweight and flabby. So you either enroll at a health spa or go on the latest diet that promises "out of this world results" in "double-quick" time. Invariably, for one reason or another, the enthusiasm dies and you find yourself back at your old lifestyle. Formal exercise is forgotten and you're back with those scrumptious desserts again. This is known as being on the diet treadmill. It's agony. You diet or exercise (or both!) for a few weeks, lose weight, shape up somewhat, only to eventually become despondent over the whole thing, give up in disgust, and of course, let that old flab creep back on. . .did I say *creep* back on? No way! It springs back into position like a bow-string releasing an arrow, and settles into your midsection as though it should never have left. You know the situation. . . .

So you carry on for a few weeks or months, until a chance remark or observation prompts you to start all over again. Your enthusiasm is rekindled. You psyche yourself up to really making an all-time effort. You mean well—but the dreaded up-down "yo-yo" sequence is virtually impossible to beat. Pretty soon, you're back to square one—and depressed again.

Modern statistics show that less than 1% of all would-be reducers ever really cure obesity. The other 99% just go up and down on the diet treadmill, or worse, they continue to gain more and more as the years go on and on. . . . .

Here's an important point to remember. Don't let anyone tell you that it is normal for the body to carry large amounts of fat and blubber. Nature originally intended us to be trim and functionally athletic. It is by overeating (especially the overeating of the wrong foods), that our body has no choice but to store the excess energy as fat. Overeating and underexercising, that is! Two of the most common sins against nature.

How long did it take you to get fat and out of condition—five, ten, or fifteen *years?* Well, don't expect to return to an ideal weight in five, ten or fifteen *days.* It can't be done. You *will* notice a difference after even this short period, but for significant results, you need longer. Give it a chance.

Necessity may be the mother of invention. But we have developed this book for you out of a need, not a necessity. A perfect figure is hardly a necessity in this day and age. In fact, 99.9% of today's men and women get on quite well with their flabby, ill-conditioned bodies. Life is designed to accommodate *them!* Clothes come in out-sized sizes. Housework is less demanding each decade. Cars are available to reduce the hazards of having to use our limbs in walking to the local store; and garages for those cars are built into our very dwelling places to reduce our energy output to *reach* them! Driving is made easier by the advent of power steering and so on. . .Life is easier and less strenuous, so who wants a firm, well-conditioned, slim fat-free body? Who *needs* it? No one! Who *wants* it? Everyone!

Why should you make an effort to have a dynamic body-shape? You may be happy as you are. . .but are you? That's the whole point. Whether you are currently excessively thin and scrawny or fat and flabby, *you want to look better.* Otherwise you wouldn't read this far. You know deep down in your heart that the only alternative to acting positively for an improved bodyshape is not to act at all. And that means resigning yourself to staying the way you look and feel at present, with the distinct possibility of further deterioration as the years go by!

So don't ever underestimate the *real* joy of being shapely. It's not just the sense of knowing that you look above average, or that you are sexier looking and more appealing. There are bonuses. You will gain enormous satisfaction from knowing that you are fitter and statistically have a better chance of surviving the ills that accompany the obese and undernourished. (Insurance figures indicate that life expectancy decreases with the increased amount of fat a person carries.)

It is your inherited right to daydream about the kind of bodyshape you want to develop. Naturally, your ultimate shape achieved will depend on such things as metabolism, bone structure, whether or not you have been fat as a child (in which case you may have more fat-cells, making it harder to lose every single ounce of fat), organic and glandular health, age and individual capacity for formal exercise. Accordingly, before starting this or any other diet and exercise program you should ask your doctor's opinion, get a complete physical stress-test and show him this book. Chances are he'll be delighted that you are going to do something positive for your body. But it is always better to get a doctor's "go ahead" before starting anything new that involves your physical well-being.

Now is the time to decide to go ahead with this plan. Daydream by all means. Does any TV or film celebrity have the type of body you want? Well, now you have something to aim for. . .and unless you have some abnormal or inherited condition. . .What's to stop you from attaining *your* dream?

Chapter 2

LEARN FROM THE PROFESSIONALS

Have you ever seen any of those professional musclebuilding types on TV? You know, the guys with huge shoulders, enormous chests and tiny, waspish waists. You could be forgiven for thinking of them as freaks because they have such tremendous muscle-size combined with the minimum of fat. Likewise with the professional woman beauty contestant. Fantastic bosoms, small waistlines, and absolutely no ugly fat. Both these groups of people have an identical secret. You may not want to look like Mr. Universe, nor may you want a 40-inch bustline going steady with the 21-inch waist of a Miss World. Nevertheless, you can apply the *professional know-how* of both the beauty-contest women and the professional musclemen to your own case. In a more moderate way, of course.

Necessity is the mother of invention, and because both bodybuilders and beauty contestants *have* to have shapely, fat-free bodies to win approval from the judges at their respective contests, both have become experts in shaping the human body, keeping trim, and *entirely* void of unsightly fat. These pros are ever aware of two points where building a dynamic bodyshape is concerned:

1. That exercise without diet is useless.
2. That diet without exercise is useless.

If you want to develop an attractive bodyshape, whether you are currently *overweight* or scrawnily *underweight*, you must apply both exercise and diet to correct and normalize your bodyweight, and to help in regaining line and proportion, all of which combine to form an exciting new physical appearance.

Diet is necessary because:
It controls the calories ingested by the body and is *the only way* to reduce bodyweight significantly, quickly and safely.

Exercise is necessary because:
It tones your muscles, helps hold a better energy level and adds shape and contour to the body.

As I said, pro bodybuilders and beauty queens really know the secrets of ridding the body of fat and adding extra "line" to their appearance. Their very existence depends on it. Now you can learn and apply these principles in a more moderate way, to remold *your* body to more desirable and sexually attractive proportions.

With regard to the diet, it should not really be referred to as a diet. I am simply recommending that you change your style of eating as a permanent part of your life.

It is possible that your eating at present is faulty, in that it may not be balanced either in food ingredients or in actual quantity in relation to your specific requirements. Faulty nutrition is common. It is typified by any diet that is loaded with carbohydrates, sugars, starches and fats. For example, if you make a regular habit of eating more sugars and starches than your body can immediately utilize, some are converted to the short storage starch known as glycogen, which can be quickly reconverted to glucose when your body needs energy.

However, most of the excess carbohydrates you eat may be converted directly to fat. Bodyshape professionals know and apply these important nutritional principles so that they work for them!

Formal exercise is the "bug-bear" of society today. Most people abhor it, loathe it and scoff at its importance. Sir Winston Churchill was quoted as saying, "When I have a sudden urge to indulge in strenuous physical exercise, I lie down until the feeling goes away. . . ."

Modern man is incredibly inactive. He gets up in the morning to clean his teeth with an electric toothbrush, shaves with an electric razor, lounges in his car going to work, sits at an office desk, at a coffee break, at dinner and eventually in front of the TV before taking a hot bath and finally retiring to bed.

There are many facts and fallacies about exercise, of what it can and cannot do for your body.

One misconception is that a little bit of exercise will take off a lot of fat. For example, many people think that if you adopt a regular habit of doing 20 sit-ups each night before you go to bed (or each morning, if you like) that their fat tummy will miraculously disappear. This is just not so. Exercise has to be of a very vigorous and extensive nature to bring about an overall fat loss. For instance, it takes about 15 hours to walk off a pound of fat. It has been established that, whereas moderate exercise may be helpful to some individuals in giving them added vigor and muscle tone, the idea of "spot" reducing a certain area by doing sit-ups for tummy, or squats for thighs and hips, is largely erroneous.

Formal exercise is a desirable ingredient, but is not necessary for a reduction in fatty body weight. Plenty of exercise can contribute to a significant expenditure of calories, which in turn can lead to a weight loss, but it is your diet that is principally responsible.

Exercise (of the right kind) is extremely valuable. Not only does it tone the muscles, firming them up to an attractive "tonus" condition, but it also gives those muscles that extra sleekness in line (particularly noticeable when combined with sensible eating habits). There is also the benefit to the respiratory and cardio-vascular system, which is important for the full utilization of oxygen and complete functional fitness.

It may have occured to you to join a commercial gym in your area. One should beware of spending a lot of money for near useless facilities.

Whereas there are many reputable commercial gyms throughout the world, there are also numerous establishments which are really worthless.

In the initial stages, one can be subjected to huge membership fees and even then find that many of the gym's facilities come under a special heading which requires even further expense. Many of these commercial gym organizations have "plush" surroundings, such as wall-to-wall carpeting, soft music, chrome-plated fixtures and fittings, electrical vibrator machines, sauna baths, sun rooms, eucalyptus rooms, and so on. All *look* very nice, yet actually *do* very little. Other health clubs (sometimes known as body shops) are nothing more than commercial grab-the-money-and-run operations which change ownership almost as often as towels. The unscrupulous organizations will advertise free days of full gym facilities. When you arrive, you may get a five minute "show around" and a fifteen minute high-pressure sell, coupled with a wealth of semi-phony discount offers. It is advised that you tread carefully when selecting any type of commercial gym organization. It should be added, of course, that there *are* many gyms which give a good service for a moderate and fair fee.

Do not sign anything until you have made several comparisons. Ask various friends who are members whether or not the benefits they derive are worth the fee involved.

Remember, if there are a preponderance of "roller" electric reducing or vibrator machines at an establishment which the management claim will help you lose fat, then that particular "spa" may not be wholly genuine. Vibrators and other electrical apparatus do not work in reducing weight. (A.M.A. 1970, Health Quackery Devices.)

This book shows you how to obtain bodyshape and fitness without incurring the expense of joining a gym. All our movements are designed to be performed in the comfort of your own home.

Chapter 3

KNOWING THE ENEMY

One of the first things you need to do is to assess your present appearance. This is not always simply a matter of glancing in your bedroom mirror. Very few people indeed can see themselves as they actually are. We have to know the enemy. We must know what we have to fight. Are our arms too thin? Do we suffer from bad posture? Is that fat on our hips and upper thighs? Do my calves need more shape?

How do we know, for example, if we *are* fat?

This may sound like a rather stupid question, yet surprisingly enough, many fat people are totally unaware of their condition. Sometimes it takes a remark or a photograph to bring the truth or realization that one is obese. Even some grotesquely fat people feel that they are only *slightly* overweight, or pleasantly plump. Conversely, there are a huge number of people who are carrying no more than a barely visible extra thickness of skin who feel they are totally obese and unattractive!

If you can't be objective when looking in the mirror, then you can check your degree of fatness by a simple "pinch" or "skinfold" test. This is best done at the back of the upper arm, midway between the elbow and the shoulder (the triceps).

Medical scientists use special calipers to get an accurate reading of skinfold thickness, but you can get a pretty accurate account of whether you are fat or not by simply pinching (gently) the skin at the triceps with your thumb and forefinger. The combined skin thickness and fat immediately beneath should be between one quarter to one-half an inch in breadth.

If it measures greater than an inch, you are fat! You may also perform the pinch test on your waist, hips, bottom, calf, or thigh, but the most accurate site is generally considered to be the *triceps* area. A 1970 survey by the National Health Organization (Canada) showed that the average triceps (right arm) skinfold of men is .511 inch (⅓ centimeter) and that it thickens with age from .433 inch (1.1 cm) at ages 18-24 years to .55 inch (¼ cm) between 25-44 years of age. Women's right arm triceps skinfold tests showed a consistently thicker measurement. The average

MINIMUM TRICEPS SKINFOLD THICKNESS INDICATING OBESITY (Inches (Millimeters)

AGE (YEARS)	MALES	FEMALES
5	0.4724 (12)	0.55118 (14)
6	0.4724 (12)	0.59055 (15)
7	0.5118 (13)	0.62992 (16)
8	0.55118 (14)	0.66929 (17)
9	0.59055 (15)	0.70866 (18)
10	0.62992 (16)	0.78740 (20)
11	0.66929 (17)	0.82677 (21)
12	0.70866 (18)	0.86614 (22)
13	0.70866 (18)	0.90551 (23)
14	0.66926 (17)	0.90551 (23)
15	0.62992 (16)	0.94488 (24)
16	0.59055 (15)	0.98425 (25)
17	0.55118 (14)	1.02362 (26)
18	0.59055 (15)	1.06299 (27)
19	0.59055 (15)	1.06299 (27)
20	0.62992 (16)	1.10236 (28)
21	0.66929 (17)	1.10236 (28)
22	0.70866 (18)	1.10236 (28)
23	0.70866 (19)	1.10236 (28)
24	0.74803 (20)	1.10236 (28)
25	0.7874 (20)	1.14173 (29)
26	0.7874 (20)	1.14173 (29)
27	0.82677 (21)	1.14173 (29)
28	0.86614 (22)	1.14173 (29)
29	0.86614 (22)	1.14173 (29)
30–50	0.90551 (23)	1.1811 (30)

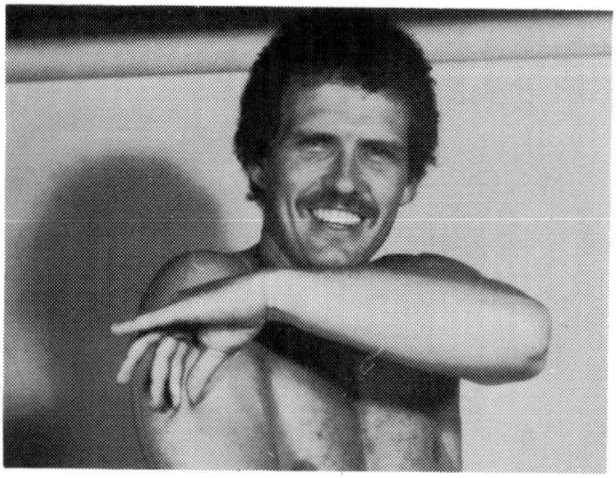

was .866 inch (2.2 cm) as young adults, women average .708 inch (1.8 cm) and at middle age they averaged .984 inch (2.5 cm). Here is a skinfold obesity chart. You may like to ask your spouse or a close friend to measure your triceps skinfold thickness, since there is sometimes a tendency to cheat when one takes the measurement oneself.

YOUR NORMAL WEIGHT SHOULD BE. . . . . . .

Height/Weight tables are really only a rough guide. Your best way to tell if you are overweight is as we suggested earlier. Take a skinfold reading at the triceps of the arm. It could well happen that a sedentary worker could test his or her weight against height according to this table and still be fat, and, on the other hand a field athlete could "register" an overweight condition by comparing himself with the chart and yet not have any significant fat on his entire body.

Your main guide should be the triceps skinfold test and your bedroom mirror. However, we are including a much used height/weight table for both sexes so that you may see how you presently compare. Just remember that they are not necessarily indicative of exactly how much you should weigh in order to be a perfect physical specimen.

Your weight may coincide with the following height/ weight scales. Yet you may feel that you still don't have

HEIGHT/WEIGHT FEMALE

Height**	Small Frame		Medium Frame		Large Frame	
In. Cm.	Lb.	Kg.	Lb.	Kg.	Lb.	Kg.
6'0" - 182.9	138-147	62.6-67.0	144-159	65.3-72.1	153-173	69.4-78.5
5'11"- 180.3	134-144	60.8-65.3	140-155	63.5-70.3	149-168	67.6-76.2
5'10"- 177.8	130-140	59.0-63.5	136-151	61.7-68.5	145-163	65.8-74.0
5' 9"- 175.3	126-135	57.2-61.2	132-147	59.9-66.7	141-158	64.0-71.7
5' 8"- 172.7	121-131	54.9-59.4	128-143	58.1-64.9	137-154	62.1-69.9
5' 7"- 170.2	118-127	53.5-57.6	124-139	56.2 63.1	133-150	60.3-68.1
5' 6"- 167.6	114-123	51.7-55.8	120-135	54.4-61.2	129-146	58.5-66.2
5' 5"- 165.1	111-119	50.3-54.0	116-130	52.6-59.0	125-142	56.7-64.4
5' 4"- 162.6	108-116	49.0-52.6	113-126	51.3-57.2	121-138	54.9-62.6
5' 3"- 160.0	105-113	47.6-51.3	110-122	49.9-55.3	118-134	53.5-60.8
5' 2"- 157.5	102-110	46.3-49.9	107-120	48.5-54.2	115-131	52.2-59.4
5' 1"- 154.9	99-107	44.9-48.5	104-116	47.2-52.6	112-128	50.8-58.1
5' 0"- 152.4	96-104	45.3-47.2	101-113	45.8-51.3	109-125	49.4-56.7
4'11"- 149.8	94-101	42.6-45.8	98-110	44.4-49.9	106-122	48.1-55.3
4'10"- 147.3	98-98	41.7-44.4	96-107	43.5-48.5	104-119	47.2-54.0

* For women between 18 and 25, subtract 1 pound for each year under 25.

** With shoes with 2 inches.

HEIGHT/WEIGHT MALE

Height***.	Small Frame	Medium Frame	Large Frame
6'4"- 193.0	164-175 74.4-79.4	172-190 78.0-86.2	182-204 82.6-92.6
6'3"- 190.5	160-171 72.6-77.6	167-185 75.3-83.9	178-199 80.8-90.3
6'2"- 188.0	156-167 70.8-75.8	162-180 73.5-81.7	173-194 78.5-88.0
6'1"- 185.4	152-162 69.0-73.5	158-175 71.7-79.4	168-189 76.2-85.8
6'0"- 182.9	148-159 67.1-71.8	154-170 69.9-77.1	164-184 74.4-83.5
5'11"-180.3	144-154 65.3-69.9	150-165 68.1-74.9	159-179 72.1-81.2
5'10"-177.8	140-150 63.5-68.1	146-160 66.2-72.6	155-174 70.3-78.9
5' 9"-175.3	136-145 61.7-65.8	142-156 64.4-70.3	151-170 68.5-77.1
5' 8"-172.7	132-141 59.9-64.0	138-152 62.6-69.0	147-166 66.7-75.3
5' 7"-170.2	128-137 58.1-62.1	134-147 60.8-66.7	142-161 64.4-73.0
5'6"- 167.6	124-133 56.2-60.3	130-143 59.0-64.9	138-156 62.6-70.8
5'5"- 165.1	121-129 54.9-58.5	127-139 57.6-63.1	135-152 61.2-69.0
5'4"- 162.6	118-126 53.5-57.2	124-136 56.2-61.7	132-148 59.9-67.1
5'3"- 160.0	115-123 52.2-55.8	121-133 54.9-60.3	129-144 58.5-65.3
5'2"- 157.5	112-121 50.8-54.6	118-129 53.5-58.5	126-141 57.2-64.0

*** With shoes with 1 inch heels.

perfect bodyshape. If, after careful analysis you feel that you are still either too thin or too fat, then you can continue with this bodyshaping program until you get to the shape you are aiming for. Both height/weight scales listed above are only a rough guide.

You may have heard of the term "spot reducing." The phrase was devised to denote the ability of specific exercises to reduce certain areas. For example, sit-ups are *supposed* to reduce the tummy, leg movements are *supposed* to take fat off the legs, and hip exercises are *supposed* to take flab off the hips. . .but they do not work that way. Specific exercises *shape, tone,* and *firm up* individual muscles areas, but they do not take off fat from the area. Exercise only removes fat on an overall basis by virtue of burning up calories. The term "spot reducing" is a misnomer.

Both men and women tend to have the same figure problems, even though ultimately they are aiming at different shapes.

Your task is to assess the job that has to be done in *your* case.

1. Arrange your bathroom mirror so that you can check your posture from the side. If you are upright and have an alert stance, then you don't appear to have a problem. A sloppy stance means that you will have to straighten up, and perhaps do some of our special postural exercises.

2. Check (by pinching between thumb and forefinger or with calipers) if you are carrying much fat on the inside of your knees, lower back, hips, triceps (upper arm) and waist. Excessive fat on any of these places indicates that you should alter your thermodynamic balance. In other words, exercise more and eat less.

3. Your ideal shape will be typified by a relatively fat free body (bony wrists, knees, etc.) and an attractive shapely line. Both men and women should have torso and limbs that have plenty of individual curves and line. A fatty covering fills in the recesses of your body and detracts from the overall shapeliness. A fat-free body has more curves, more shape and more sex appeal.

4. If you are one of those lucky people who appear to be slightly underweight, then we have the happy news of telling you that you can eat, eat, eat. Plus, we will detail a specific weight gaining regime to help add those vital pounds.

PART II

EXERCISE–BEGINNERS AND ADVANCED

Chapter 4

OH NO! EXERCISES

If you are like most people, chances are you will not really like the look of this program. I am sure you will have noticed by now that you will be doing *exercises.* "Oh No!" I can hear you saying in utter dismay. "I hate exercising and besides, I don't have time."

Well, hate exercising you may, but I'm not so willing to accept the "I don't have time" story. If you genuinely can't find a few minutes each day to do something that can benefit you enormously, then it's probably time you took stock of your life style and did a little reorganizing here and there. For those of you who hate exercising, give it a try one more time. Start with a short ten minute workout which we have suggested in this course. Don't go all out. Don't strain. Take it easy at first. Gradually, as the days go by, you will be able to do the harder exercises. Soon you will start to look forward to your mini-workouts. Exercise is necessary for a good, strong, healthy, virile life. You cannot possibly enjoy everlasting zest and vigor if you choose to ignore the power of regular exercise. Exercise can lift your spirits, relieve tension and make the day's work easier to do. When critical "weak" moments in your diet come, exercise can renew your enthusiasm. If you have, in the past, bought a publication on slimming or fitness, then you will probably have been given a program of literally dozens of different exercises, all for different, obscure body parts. If you were to do all these exercises at one time you would probably end up in bed for a week. Besides, your exercise session would take several hours, at best. It is with this problem in mind, and my awareness that most people dislike formal exercise, that I have developed my own super mini-routines which work the larger areas of the body, and work them hard! These exercises that I have compiled into mini-workouts concentrate on the large "trouble" areas of your figure. They are, in my opinion, far superior to all those flimsy, arm-waving, leg twisting type of calisthenics that most "diet and exercise" publications recommend. Why? Because my exercises (although not all new in themselves) are designed to "pound" your fat away. They are grisly, possibly awkward, tough movements, as opposed to the kind that are artistic, dainty, graceful and next to useless when compared to the high-powered calorie-burning movements I advocate. My mini-routines are designed to give you maxi-results in the least possible time. Even though they are high-powered, you women will not gain huge muscles. Simply follow my routines with the correct recommended diet principles, and your fat will gradually melt away. These routines are for the underweights too!

How do I know? Because my fat burning system, which recommends a tailored diet in conjunction with my special mini-exercise program, has recently been used by scores of people of almost every physical type. The results have amazed everyone but me. I knew from the beginning that my plan would work. When you burn up more calories with my system than you ingest, you simply have to lose flabby body weight. In fact, it would be the same for any basically sound system. There are no two ways about it. Follow my plan to the letter; you will lose weight, and at the same time, look better and feel more fit for it! Not only that, but the reduction of fat around your eyes, jowls, mouth and neck may well make your face appear younger looking. This is one of the comments I receive time after time. Invariably, a goodly reduction in weight may give your face back its youthful appearance. You're younger looking, and people will notice!

I have two routines for you: one is the *Beginner's Mini-Workout* and the other is the *Advanced Mini-Workout.* If you are an average woman or man who hasn't been exercising vigorously of late, then start with the beginner's routine. You will gradually condition yourself so that after a short while, you will be able to move on to the Advanced Mini-Workout.

Remember these four points for success.

1. Always perform as many "counts" of an exercise (going up and down during a floor dip as one "count," for example) as possible without straining. When a movement gets really hard to do, then stop that particular exercise.
2. Don't exercise when cold. Wear loose clothing that doesn't restrict movement. Only exercise naked or in a swim costume when the temperature is distinctly warm. To exercise when the body is chilled could lead to minor strains.
3. The best time to exercise is usually in late afternoon or early evening. However, any time is good so long as you wait at least an hour after a meal before throwing yourself into a workout. It is a good idea, however, to try and exercise approximately the same time each day. This gives your body time to adapt to regular exercise and thus prepare your built-in energy "clock" for physical activity at your regular workout time.
4. It is important to realize that these exercise routines are designed to be used by individuals who are either *overweight* or *underweight.* The governing factor in whether or not one gains or loses weight is not dependent on what formal exercises one does, but almost entirely on the *amount* of *calories one ingests.*

Chapter 5

BEGINNER'S MINI ROUTINE

Here are the exercises:

MINI-ROUTINE NO. 1(Beginners)

Skip-Jogging(a)
(Warm-up and overall calorie burner)

This exercise is not hard. Simply run in place. You may adopt a skipping type movement if you wish, only without the use of a skipping rope. It is often a good idea to perform this exercise to the rousing "beat" of a well-liked pop song.

Perform up to three minutes of this exercise. Much less if you are really out of condition. One minute is quite long enough if you're 40 pounds overweight.

(a)

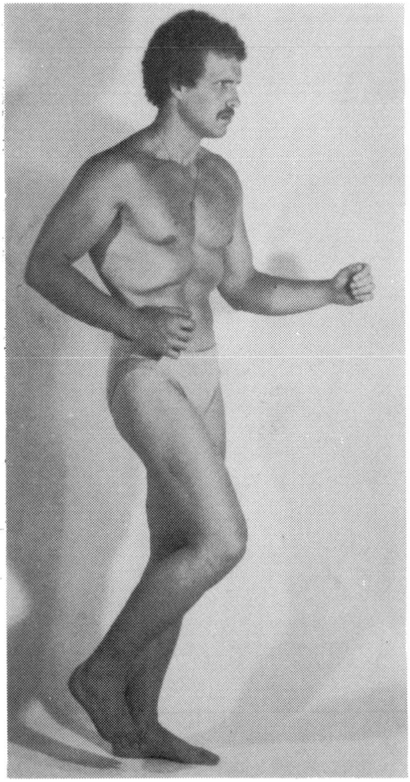

Squat(b)
(Thighs and hips)

1. Place a thick book on floor under heels. Stand upright with arms out in front to help balance.
2. Lower slowly into the squat position as illustrated (b) until thighs are parallel with floor. Return to standing position and repeat.
3. Take care to breathe deeply during the movement. "In" on the way down, and "Out" on the way up.

Perform 6-15 counts.

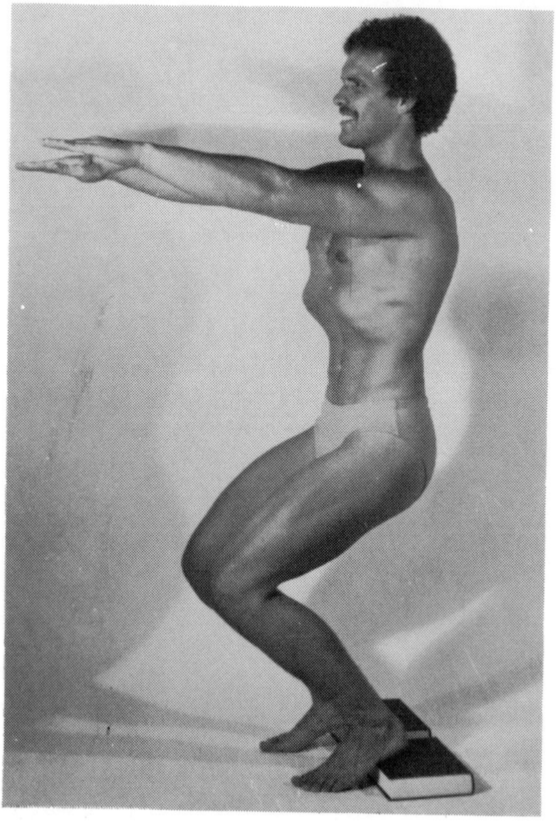

(b)

Table Dip(c)
(Chest, shoulders and arms)

Adopt a position as shown in illustration (top). Make sure that neither your feet nor the table are so placed that they may slip. Lower your torso to the table by bending the arms only. Straighten and repeat.

Perform 5-10 complete "counts".

(c)

Calf Raise(d)
(Lower legs)

Stand with feet 6 inches apart. Raise up on toes to stretch as high as possible. Continue this "up-down" movement until calves are burning slightly.

You may hold on to the back of a chair should you find difficulty in balancing.

Perform from 15-20 counts.

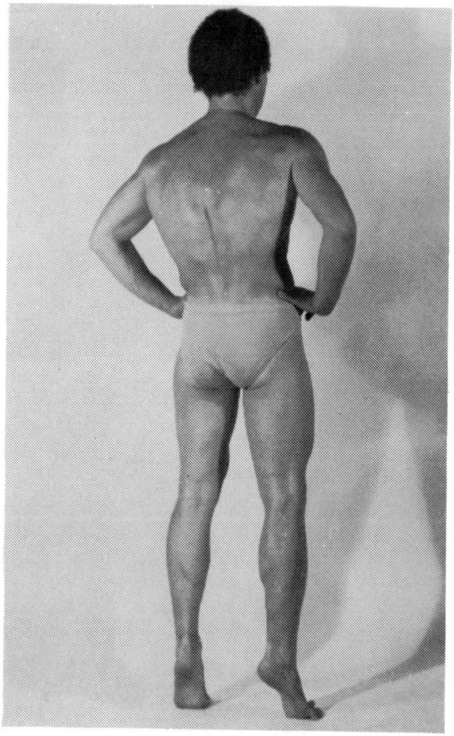

(d)

(d)

Side Twists(e)
(Midsection)

It's best to stand facing a mirror if possible for this one. Fold arms and face straight ahead, legs about 15 inches apart. Commence exercise by twisting the upper body *only* from side to side.

Keep face looking straight ahead at all times. Do not allow the hips to twist during the movement. The exercise involves only the quick twisting of the torso and folded arms.

Like exercise (a), you may find this more enjoyable to perform to fast-paced music. Continue for up to one minute.

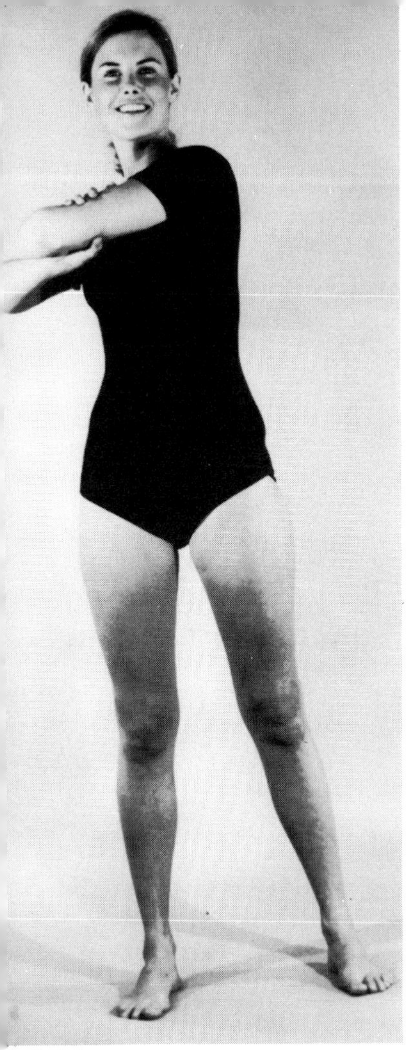

(e)

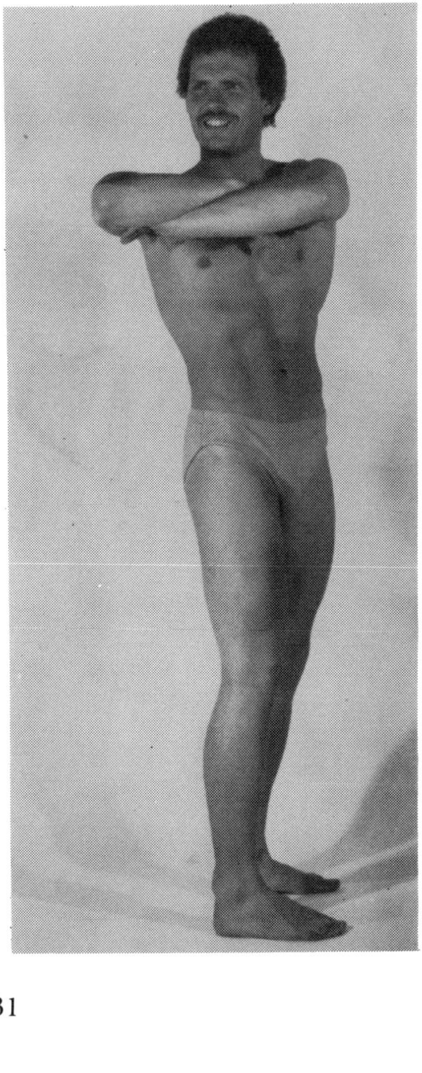

Chapter 6

ADVANCED MINI-ROUTINE

High Knee Running in Place (1)
(Warm-up and general calorie burner)

Run in place. After you have gotten used to this movement, aim to lift the knees higher and higher for each repetition.

Perform from 3-10 minutes.

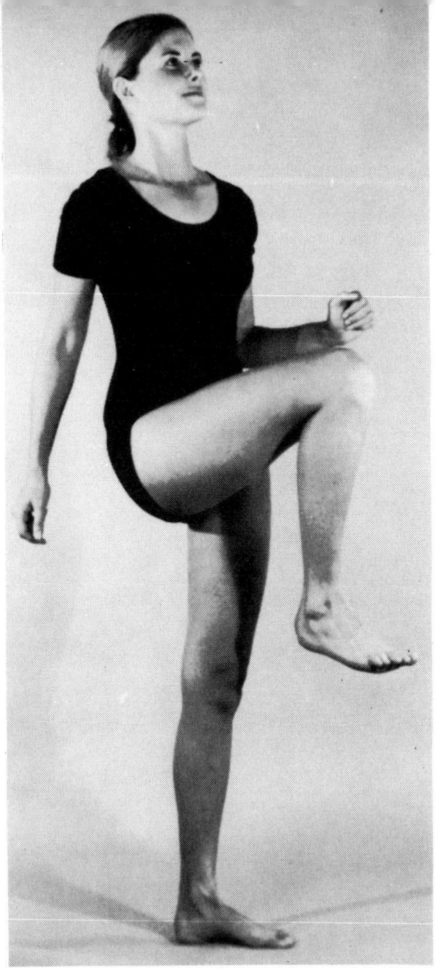

(1)

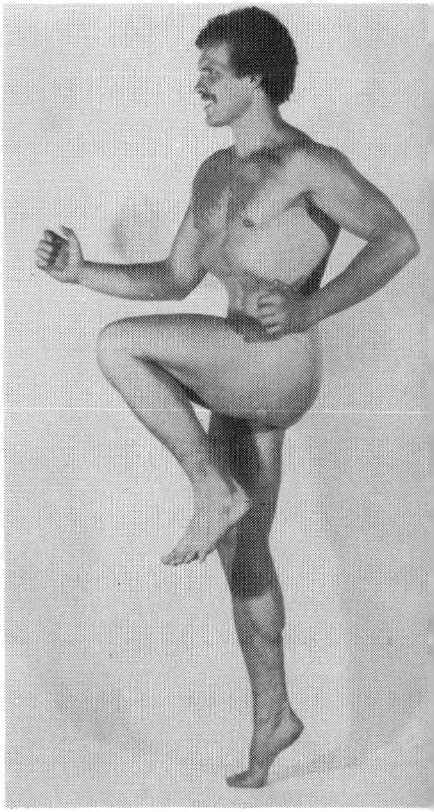

Sissy Squat (2)

(Thighs, calves and hips)

Stand erect, hands on hips, feet about 8 inches apart. Now lower the body into a squat position so that the thighs are parallel to the ground. The main "trick" to this exercise is to lean back throughout the movement. Heels must leave the ground with hips forward as illustrated. You may hold on to the back of a chair for balance in this movement.

Perform 10-25 counts.

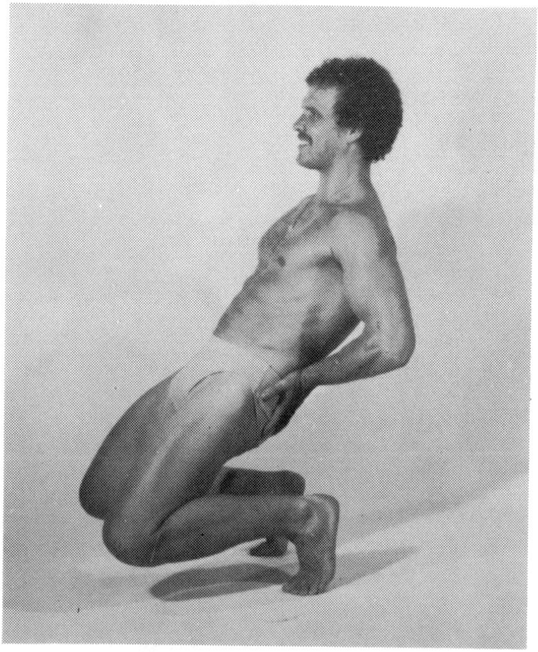

(2)

Floor Dips (3)
(Chest, shoulders and arms)

Adopt a position as illustrated. Lower chest to floor by bending arms. Push up while maintaining a straight body. Elbows should point outwards when lowering the body.

Should you find this dipping movement beyond your capabilities, then place a cushion or pillow under the knees and simply perform the exercise while resting on the floor. This is far easier. Nevertheless, aim ultimately to master the correct way of doing this movement.

Try 6-12 counts.

(3)

Calf Raise on Book (4)
(Lower legs)

Stand with toes placed on a large book (telephone directory). Lower heels to floor and raise up on toes to stretch as high as possible. Continue this "up-down" movement until calves are burning slightly.
Perform from 20-30 counts.

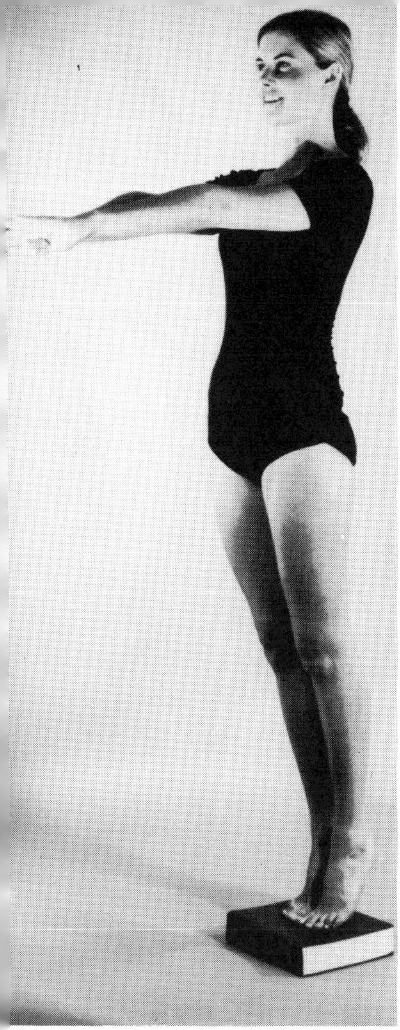

(4)

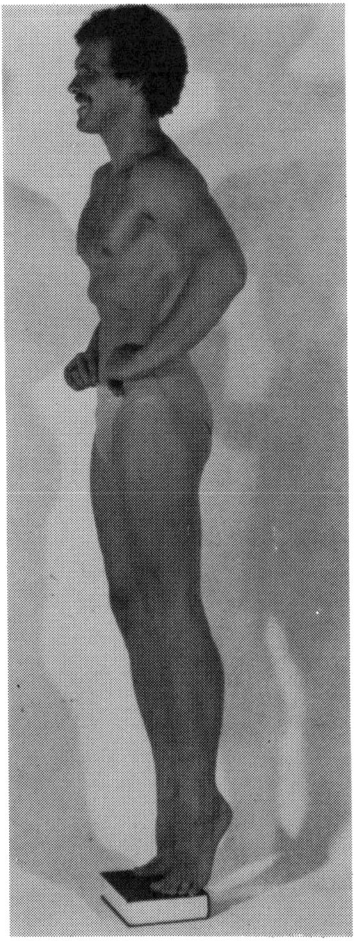

Broomstick Twists (5)
(General mid-section)

Place a broomstick behind shoulders as illustrated. Stand with feet comfortably apart. Twist from side to side. Keep hips fairly still (and facing forward) throughout the movement.

Perform 50 to 100 counts.

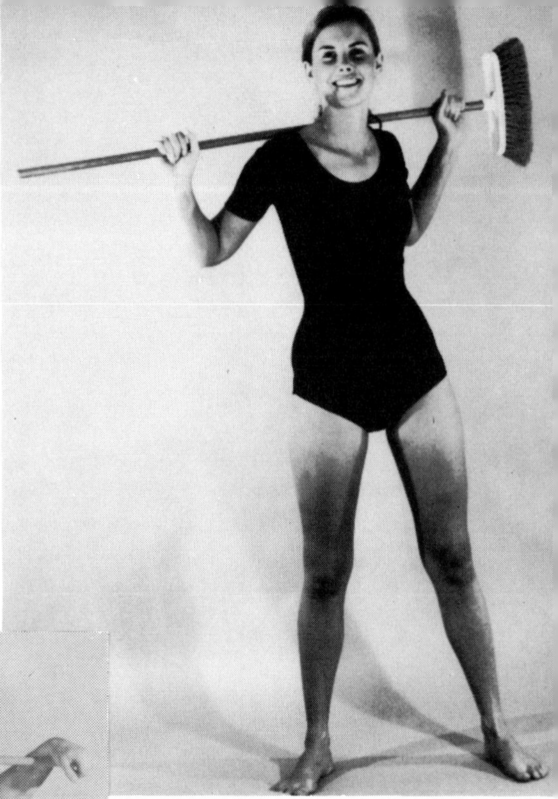

(5)

Chapter 7

YOUR HEALTH

A great bodyshape appearance may seem to be a vital thing to you because you are anxious to impress others, and to be admired. But there is another factor involved. Your health.

Outward physical appearance is not necessarily indicative of inward well being, but it is often a good guide.

There are a few health rules that apply to all of us.

Smoking

Smoking is best cut out completely. Apart from the unpleasant stale smell tobacco gives the smoker, it has been conclusively proven that cigarette smoking is one of the main causes of heart disease and lung cancer, two of the greatest killers of our time. If you find that you are unable to give up smoking, keep trying. The very fact that you are reading this shows that you have some interest in improving your health and figure. So why not make up your mind to smoke no more?

How many people would use the services of an airline company if they were told that one in seven of the company's planes crashed, leaving no survivors? When you smoke a cigarette, the chances are that you decrease your life expectancy three times the length of time it took you to smoke the cigarette.

Alcohol

Drinking is another negative step away from health and

fitness. Naturally, moderate drinkers may not suffer ill effects, but if your drinking is becoming a daily practice, and if you find that you miss it if a day goes by without a drink, then it may be time to consider cutting down, or even stopping all together.

Most alcoholic drinks are relatively high in "empty" calories, and will do nothing for aiding overall physical appearance.

Pills and Drugs

It should be unnecessary to mention the harm that regular prescription pill taking may do to the system; sleeping pills, aspirin, diet pills, headache pills, and the like. All foreign matter (to the body) should be taken only with full knowledge and sanction of your doctor.

Where drugs such as "hash", "grass" and cocaine are concerned, never listen to stories about them being safe because they are "natural". The poppy is a natural flower, but it gives vent to one of the human bodies greatest enemies—heroin.

Your rule for healthful living is to eat foods which are wholesome, nutritious and as unprocessed as possible. Fresh food is preferred to canned, such as fresh vegetables, fresh milk, meat, fish, eggs, fruit. Most preserved or canned products contain additives, preservatives and coloring. Governments are just disclosing that some of these ingredients that have been used for years may be cancer forming. *Now* they tell us!

Take no chances. . . .

Fresh air and sunshine

Getting some daily fresh air is highly recommended. City dwellers may find this difficult, but most big towns have a park or a lake where the air, if not perfect, is certainly purer than the downtown areas.

If you have a job that involves a great deal of night work, then try to get out in the sun for a few minutes to rejuvenate yourself. Natural light is very important to the overall health of the body. In some people excessive sunbathing can cause skin problems sometimes of a serious nature. Because the sun is responsible for all life, you need a regular dose for health and strength.

Stress Control

Worry is a killer. Endeavor to organize your life so that you are not burdened by excessive nervous stress. Tackle problems as they come up. Never let them mount up so that life becomes unbearable. If your children, job, housework or financial situation is making you a nervous wreck, then sort out the problem in your mind, decide on the best way to tackle it, then act positively by following through with action. If you can't make decisions, then consult professionals who may be able to, such as lawyers, accountants, and doctors.

Chapter 8

THE PROBLEM OF BEING TOO THIN

Many people envy the naturally skinny person. "Oh, that I should have your problem" are words that many underweight individuals hear with regularity. Yet, it gives them no comfort. They feel they are no more than skin and bones, and to a person, they want one thing, more weight! Men want added muscular impressiveness. Women want those attractive, sexy curves and feminine fullness.

The first point the underweight person should realize is that all added flesh should be firm and toned. You are totally defeating your purpose by just willfully wishing for *any* type of extra weight.

Every pound that you add to your frame *has* to be in the right place. Additional *avoirdupois*, in the wrong place, will detract from your appearance. There are many superficially skinny people who have worsened their appearance by deliberately eating scores of cookies, pastries, and enormous amounts of sugar products, with the net result of having added ugly fat to hips, thighs, knees and waist areas.

There are no two ways about it; the underweight person should increase weight by eating wholesome foods in conjunction with a sensible program of planned exercise. This will ensure some degree of tone in the new poundage gained.

You may feel that you have tried to put on weight, but failed. It is likely that you haven't tried hard enough.

You are underweight for one of four reasons:—

1. You have a light bone structure (heredity) and to be light in weight is a family trait.

2. You are not eating enough to balance your expenditure of energy.

3. You have a high metabolic rate (burning up calories). Many youngsters are characterized by high metabolisms).

4. You are living on your nerves, or otherwise suffering poor health or illness.

If you are particularly worried, or have reason to believe you are not in normal health, then of course see your doctor. As recommended earlier, we state that your doctor should be consulted anyway. Before undertaking formal exercise of any nature, you should get medical permission; show your doctor the program you intend to embark on and ask for a physical stress test.

Your three point plan for gaining weight is:

1. To exercise using the mini-routine three times a week, with at least a day's rest between each workout. For example:—Mondays, Wednesdays, and Fridays.

2. To eat more, yet smaller meals each day. It can be a good plan to eat five snacks each day rather than two or three big meals.

3. To rest, relax and sleep adequately so that added body weight has a chance to materialize.

It may be easy to fall into the habit of eating junk foods. But they won't do you any good. For your health's sake decide to adopt a plan now of eating good wholesome food rather than the common "foodless foods" that line the shelves, row after row in the supermarkets. Empty calorie foods (foods that have a preponderance of sugar, yet little real goodness) may be harmful if taken over a long period of time.

Fill up your supermarket cart with fresh fruit, vegetables, lean cuts of meat, poultry, nuts, eggs, whole wheat breads, milk, cheese, yogurt and fish.

Use honey as a sweetener.

Discipline yourself against reaching for all those sweet, gooey, white flour devitalized products. Stay away from candies and soft drinks, hot dogs and the like.

Yes, five small meals a day may help you gain the added weight you want. Never overstuff yourself when you're not hungry, but on the other hand a walk in the fresh air before a meal may be what you require to give you that important appetite. Don't allow your stomach to go without food for long periods at a time.

Relaxation

Never run when you can walk, stand when you can sit, or sit when you can lie. . . . Learn to put your feet up, or at least relax, at odd times during the day, especially immediately after meals. If your work keeps you on the move continuously, then try to slow down, at least in your mind. If your skinniness is utmost in your mind under these circumstances, then change jobs.

Do bear in mind that as one gets older, the body metabolism tends to slow down and weight is gained, sometimes more than one would wish for. . . . Many are the people who have prayed to add weight, only to find that a few years later they have reversed the situation and found themselves carrying excess poundage. . .and drastically looking for a way to lose what they once regarded as being the most prized possession in existence. . . .

Chapter 9

YOUR POSTURE

You may develop the most dynamic body shape imaginable, but it will not impress a single person if your posture is not good. Bad posture can be caused by many variables. You may just have lazy posture, which is the least serious, since it is just a matter of straightening up, holding your head and shoulders correctly and walking with an upright stance. Other abnormal curvatures of the spine can be inherited, or due to your occupation, hobby or habits, such as the wearing of high heeled shoes, or even the gaining of excess weight.

It is important that all severe cases of poor posture should be referred to your doctor. He can in turn recommend a competent specialist who can prescribe a series of individualized exercises.

Some sports or pastimes that could lend themselves to the development of poor posture include high fashion modelling, cycling, racing, close work such as bookkeeping, and even hockey.

Activities that may help posture include typing, horseback riding, ice skating, dancing, weight-training, etc. . . .

This does not mean to say that if you're an ardent racing cyclist, that you will automatically have bad posture, or that regular horseriding will give you a perfect stance. It all depends on the individual.

Good posture is personified by the alert looking individual who, when viewed from the side, standing erect, has a perfect balance of all the moveable body areas, such as the head, rib-box, pelvis, knees etc. If one were to drop a plumb line from this side view it would pass through the following points. Center of the ear, shoulder joint, hip joint, knee joint and front of the ankle.

The presence of a "pot" belly for example can throw the entire postural balance out of line. The extra weight can cause the pelvis to tilt unnaturally, which in turn may cause other areas such as the spine and head to balance awkwardly in order to compensate. In time this poor posture can become ingrained into the body appearance and may become difficult to entirely correct. Sitting is a postural position in which we spend a considerable amount of time. When you sit, make sure that the back, if properly supported, and the pelvic girdle assume the proper tilt. Don't slouch.

We spend about a third of our life sleeping, or at least lying down. Movement, growth and change occur during this time, even though we may feel nothing happening. You should pay attention to what you are lying on. A sagging mattress with grooves that have been formed by some occupant over a long period of time does not aid your posture. Firm mattresses are best.

A pillow is essential if you sleep on your side but not always necessary if you sleep on your back.

Here are three basic posture exercises. Should you have extensive postural problems, make an appointment to see an orthopedic expert. He should be able to give you tailor-made advice.

LUMBAR EXERCISE

1. Lie flat on your back. Feet straight and toes pointed up. Heels about two inches apart.
2. Grasp both your hands firmly just below right knee and pull towards chest. Keep lower back flat against mat while performing exercise.
3. Repeat with other leg.
4. Now do this exercise by grasping both knees and pulling toward chest.
   Be sure your lower back is firmly against mat.
5. Hold to a slow count of three.
6. Work up to ten times daily.

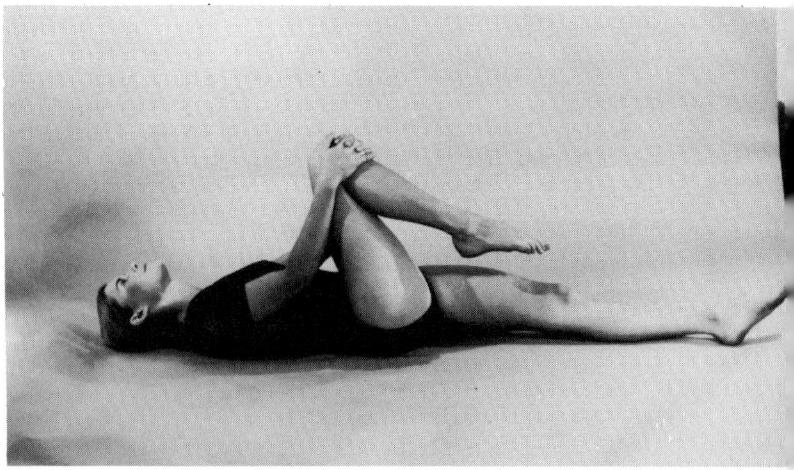

DORSAL EXERCISE

1. Lying on abdomen, place forehead on the floor.
2. Raise head and upper chest as high as you can.
3. Raise legs at the same time.
4. Clasp hands together across small of back.
5. Hold to a slow count of three.
6. Lower slowly.
7. Relax.
8. Work up to ten times daily.

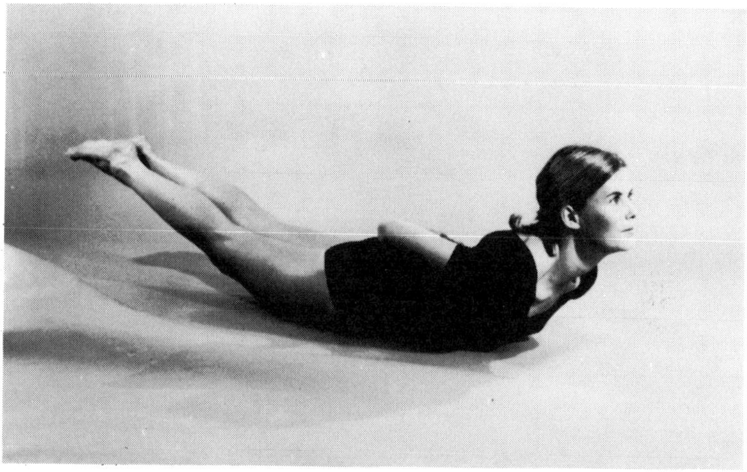

CERVICAL EXERCISE

1. Sit on a chair and clasp hands behind head, chin down.
2. Keep elbows perpendicular to head.
3. Push head gradually against the resistance of hands.
4. Hold to a slow count of three.
5. Release gradually.
6. Relax.
7. Work up to ten times daily.

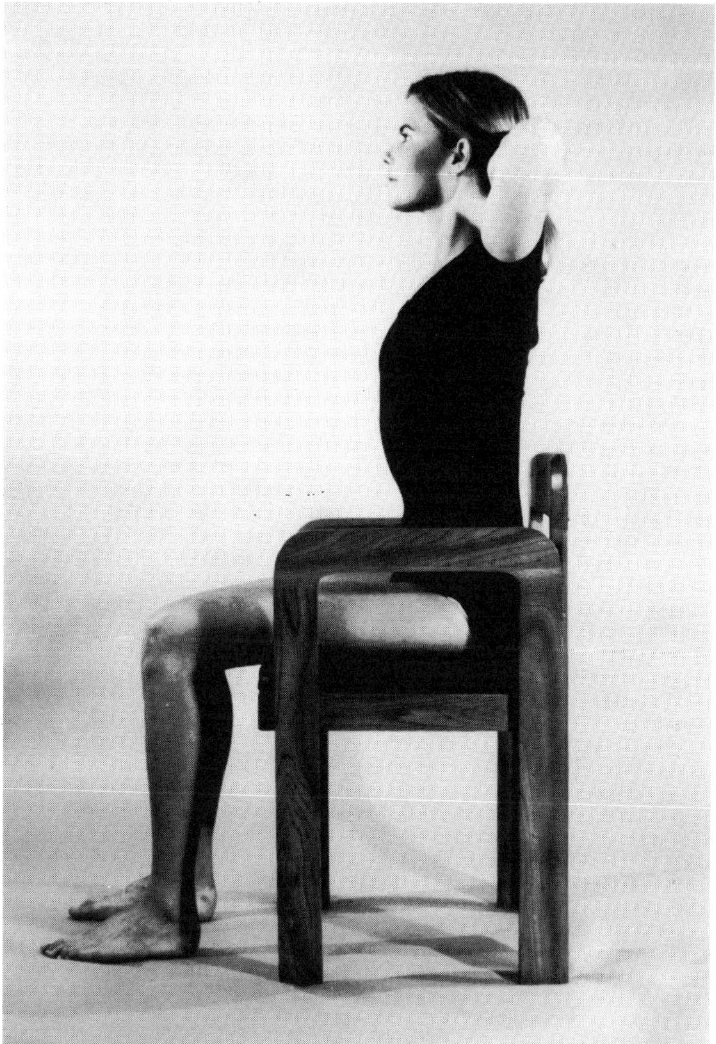

PART III

PUMPING IRON FOR MEN AND WOMEN

Star of the film "Pumping Iron," 30 year old Arnold Schwarzenegger, is the King of the Bodybuilding World and is destined to reach further stardom as an actor.

Chapter 10

PUMPING IRON FOR MEN AND WOMEN

The popularity of pumping iron (or using weights) to mold your body shape is increasing daily. Weight training, or at least the training with increased resistance has always been with us. It can be traced back to the 6th century B.C.

A young Greek named Milo commenced carrying a young bull-calf around the farmyard from the day of its birth. As he continued to do this daily, his strength would keep pace with the animals regular growth. One day he carried the full grown bull on his shoulders around the Olympic Arena in Greece to the enthusiastic cheers and praise of the crowd.

Ever since that glorious day, physical culturists have known that the "progressive overload" system of exercise built up strength, fitness and stamina, but it was only as recent as 1956 when scientific sports medical research conclusively proved that power and endurance could be built up with progressive weight training. Milo could have told them this over two thousand years ago.

Nowadays, you don't have to be a weight lifter or even a sportsperson to be able to take advantage of the health and strength benefits of weight training. In fact, using free weights remain one of the few ways left to us of keeping our muscle fully toned and fit, and of enjoying our leisure time without having to spend large sums of money.

Total beginners to "Pumping Iron," men and women alike, may want to know why weight training is such a great aid to bodyshaping. The answer is that weights are effective because the resistance (poundage) can be controlled. In other words, there will always be some demand made on the muscles, because as you get stronger you will still be able to "challenge" the muscles by increasing the weight of the exercise bar. This leads to shapelier muscles for women and bigger muscles for men.

Do women build bigger muscles if they use weights?

No! Although there may be a slight filling out of a muscle if it is *particularly* underdeveloped, women just do not get muscularly larger as a result of weight training. Their hormone balance does not allow it. With men, there is a tendency to gain muscular bodyweight. But this is a matter of personal taste. A man can control the amount of muscle he puts on his frame by reducing or adding to his overall food intake.

Is "Pumping Iron" healthy? I have heard that it is bad for the heart. If I give it up, I will automatically turn to fat and die young!

A healthy heart can only be strengthened by regular exercise. The heart is a muscle like your other muscles, equally as strong and just as capable of handling the stress brought about from heavy weight training. If you have a diseased heart, that is a different matter. Any diseased organ is unable to function perfectly under duress. For your own protection a physical stress test should be undergone before taking up weight-training or any other formal exercise.

The point of "automatically turning to fat" is another old wives tale. When one stops training there is a tendency to slowly return to how you were before you took up the training. If you were fat, you may put on weight. A thin person would usually get thinner. Also, your food intake will govern your weight when you are not involved in a training program, to a great extent. It is true that many former athletes have become fat, but this is because they have kept up their heavy eating habits developed while in full training. Obviously when you stop exercising vigorously (using up to 1000 extra calories a day) then you must also reduce your food intake from what it was during your training days.

How can a person who may be involved in strenuous work in the house or at work possibly benefit from weight lifting exercises?

Many people feel that they are active enough throughout the day. They may be involved in anything from construction work to other activities such as housework or physical labor. This question is repeatedly put to me by women who slave away in the home for numerous hours each day. They conclude with the fact that they are too tired to start doing something like "lugging barbells around." The answer of course, is that work is just that. Work. And that formal exercise is of a totally different nature. Training regularly with barbells does much more for the contouring, shaping and beautifying of a woman's figure than any type of activity she may do around the house. Training with weights leads to a curvy, intriguing, sexy figure in women and a more muscular, larger and far more attractive physical appearance in men. Whatever the work involved with either sexes, it cannot approach the results achieved with progressive resistance weight training.

When you pump iron you are performing the most concentrated type of exercise known to modern man. Each movement is designed to work a specific area of the body, and work it efficiently in a way no other form of activity can match. For example, when a woman (or man) performs ten repetitions with a 100 lb. barbell in an exercise like the squat, upon completion of the movement she will have lifted a thousand pounds in only a matter of twenty or so seconds. It is this accumulated work that tones and shapes the body. It is the repetitions of each exercise which bring about a concentrated accumulation of stress on a particular area that one is not able to obtain through any other type of exercise or general work.

It is understood that weights can build up a man's muscles but what are the limitations as far as women are concerned? The bust for example.

The bust cannot be increased in size once it has reached normal growth. The female breasts are glands, not muscles. An increase in measurement can be brought about by "insertive operations" (not recommended), pregnancy, the taking of the pill or simply by adding fat,—none of these particularly ideal ways of increasing bustline beauty. Pumping iron will firm the supporting pectoral muscles surrounding the breast, and accordingly improve the bustline appearance, even lift them, but actual glandular size increase is unlikely.

What are the fitness benefits of pumping iron? I want to feel good as well as look good.

The benefits to the body are enormous. Pumping iron is one of the very best ways of bringing out not only muscular tone and body shape, but also a degree of fitness that you may never have known since the days of your childhood and adolescence. The reason why training with weights benefits fitness is simply that weights can be tailored to your individual requirements. In other words, you use as much weight as will stimulate the skeletal muscles and overall metabolism. If you are relatively weak, then use light weights. If you are in good health and naturally strong, then you can use more substantial weight in all your exercises. Nothing is quite as perfect as modern weight training, since no one need strain at any time, when exercising with barbells or dumbells. You lift as much as you can manage using moderate effort.

Overall fitness, of course, is obtained by doing *higher* repetitions than one may normally do, and also by taking a *minimum* amount of rest between sets of exercises. For example, to maintain a degree of fitness, one has to exercise so that the rate of breathing is increased enormously, and so that the heart rate is increased and kept running at an increased beat for several minutes at a time. This can only be achieved by minimizing your rest periods and using light weights.

Can weight training help people lose weight?

The key factor in losing weight is the reduction of calories. Eating *less* food will do far more for a person wanting to lose weight than regular exercise. Regular strenuous exercise is helpful, but only when practiced in combination with a calorie-reduced diet.

The role of weight-training is mainly that of conditioning, firming and shaping the external muscles of our bodies.

What are the advantages of gym training? Is home training just as beneficial?

There are two main advantages in gym training. The first one is that a gym may have more advanced apparatus than you may have at home. Secondly, the atmosphere in a gym is more conducive to good vigorous workouts. However, one can train adequately at home if one has the willpower to do so. Basically, all one needs for training is a barbell or dumbell set, and perhaps a bench sturdy enough to hold the body in the supine position, with a supporting barbell. Many gyms charge upwards of $100 per year to as much as $1000 a year for membership. You must simply look over the facilities offered by any particular gym, and weigh the problem in your mind as to whether or not the added facilities are worth the extra money. Generally speaking, gyms that offer a large variety of electronic apparatus such as vibrator belts or other devices which they claim will help reduce fat are not the type of places that you should consider joining, since the United States and Canadian governments have officially ruled that this type of apparatus is not helpful in the permanent loss of fat from the body.

What role do weights play in improving athletic performance?

Basic weight training is used in aiding overall strength for virtually all the Olympic sports. Naturally, the actual practice of the sport is the most important thing. But pumping iron regularly is a valuable adjunct. Each sport requires a slightly different approach to the use of weights. If this is your goal, I suggest you seek out a suitable coach to aid you with an individualized schedule.

Can weight training give one added sexual virility and energy?

Pumping iron can give you extra fitness, strength and energy, but as far as changing your inherent virility, this is not likely. Failing virility may be due to age, mental conditions, organic fitness, inadequate diet or any number of medical problems. See your doctor rather than look for the solution in a barbell.

What about the age factor—When is "too old?"—and what about the youngsters?

Basically, one can make improvement with the use of weights at *any* age. It is not a matter of the chronological years, but more of your present basic condition. It is, of course, important for everyone undertaking weight training or any other strenuous activity to safeguard themselves by having a complete check-up with their doctors.

This should involve a stress test. Your doctor will then be able to decide your suitability for the type of programs that we recommend in this chapter. Some people do not have the constitutional make-up that is suitable for endurance or heavy exercise. As far as the suitability of individual people for weight training, it is not a matter of age, but more of your present condition and ability to tolerate vigorous physical exercise. It is even more important that you consult your doctor before going on this sort of program if you are currently a heavy smoker, drinker, or if you have not indulged in any regular form of exercise for some time.

With regard to youngsters, lightweight training is suitable for youngsters of all ages, if it is practiced in moderation and, of course, with resistance well within the limit of the children involved. Strenuous formal programs in weight training are not recommended for children.

It is far better that the children be encouraged to play all forms of sports—to swim, run and play games and take part in school activities of a general nature, rather than to try and get them to indulge in regular weight training. For one thing, the interest may be lacking in young children. On the other hand, playing sports lends itself more to their natural inclination towards competitive activities.

I am confused about the difference between weight lifting and weight training. Is there a difference and what is it?

The only similarity between weight lifting and weight training is that both involve the use of barbells. However, there is a fundamental difference in the way the barbells are used. The weight lifter is involved only in lifting as much weight as possible in the various movements. There are two types of weight lifting, One is called Olympic Lifting, in which the athlete is always male, and who concerns himself with just two Olympic lifts. The "Snatch" and the "Clean and Jerk". The snatch is a movement which involves the lifting from the floor to the above head position in one quick movement. The clean and jerk is a lift which involves even heavier weights, whereby the athlete pulls the weight first from the floor to his shoulders and then steadies himself to jerk or "throw" the weight up to arms length in a second movement. The other type of weight lifting is known as power lifting. This sport involves more stagnant movements. One could perhaps say that power lifting involves more strength than weight lifting, and that weight lifting involves more quick techniques rather than pure strength. The power movements are named the bench press;—a lift in which one lies on ones back on a bench and pushes the weight to arms length, the squat; a lift which involves the squatting down until the thighs are parallel to the floor, and straightening of one's legs while holding a barbell across one's shoulders; and finally the deadlift, in which the weight is lifted from the ground and held at a position where the barbell is just above the knees.

On the other hand, *weight training* is the use of barbells and dumbells to shape and condition the body. In weight training, one has very little thoughts as to the *amount* of weight being lifted. The weights in this case are utilized using repetitions from eight to twenty in shaping the muscles of the entire body.

Exactly what apparatus is needed for successful weight training? Where can I get it?

Basically, the only apparatus required in weight training is a standard barbell and dumbell set and an adjustable incline bench. You need one bar of around 5 feet in length, sufficient weight in various sizes of discs, and two dumbell rods and collars to hold the weights in place. An incline bench, which will also go into the flat position, is also a basic necessity if you want the fullest and most beneficial results from your iron pumping. These items can be obtained from specialist sport stores in most towns throughout America and Canada.

What does one wear to lift weights?

You need loose clothes—a sweatsuit is ideal, over T-shirt and shorts or swim wear, plus gym shoes. You may, of course, omit the sweatsuit in hot weather, but never train without shoes.

Choose a room with adequate ventilation, even a garage will do, and ensure that any floor standing apparatus is level and stable. Always use collars on barbells and dumbells, and make certain they are tight before commencing the exercise. Loose weights falling from a bar can cause a nasty accident.

How often should one train?

As a beginner, you should take your workouts only every other day. Never train two days in a row. Your body needs that "rest" day from strenuous exercise to recuperate and build up.

Work out three times a week, either Mondays, Wednesdays and Fridays, or Tuesdays, Thursdays and Saturdays. The choice is yours, but once made, try and stick with it.

Needless to say, if you have a cold, headache, or are just not feeling up to it, then give your training a miss. It is senseless to exercise when not feeling well. It could make you worse. On the other hand, you have to learn to differentiate between feeling genuinely tired (in which case you should go to bed) and feeling lazy. Don't let laziness stop you from working out.

I am an excessively thin man, active in numerous sports and past-times. I want desperately to add bodyweight.

You want bigger muscles? Then you must make sure that you get adequate rest and sleep. You can't expect to play tennis before you work out, and go dancing afterwards, AND gain substantial bodyweight. Your muscles must have adequate time to recuperate and build extra power. Whenever you subject your muscles to the exercises recommended in this book (or any other vigorous exercise for that matter) the muscle cells are "broken down" by the repeated tension. This tissue breakdown is what eventually causes a muscle to tire after a certain amount of strenuous exercise. However, these cells must be given rest periods to enable them to rebuild and increase overall muscle size. You must grab periods of physical relaxation whenever you can, if you want to make the very best progress in muscle building. This does not mean that you have to neglect your household duties, or quit your job. We are simply suggesting that, for optimum progress, you do not indulge in *extra* physical recreation. Learn to conserve energy. . . .Rest at all opportunities, especially after meals, if possible. The amount of sleep necessary will naturally vary from individual to individual, but as a general rule, a beginning bodybuilder should get at least eight hours sleep each night. Some may need more: others could get by on slightly less. Your muscles "build up" while you sleep.

The thin person must work out regularly and progressively, and gradually increase the amount he eats until their bodyweight starts to move upward. Many thin persons have very high metabolisms (they burn up a lot of energy, even when not doing much exercise). They must learn not to worry, to relax more, and not to waste needless energy on useless tasks.

A suggested eating schedule for the thin person would be along the following lines.

Breakfast
Orange juice
Cereal and milk
Sausage and eggs (or bacon or ham)
2 slices toast and honey
Glass of milk

Mid Morning
Glass of milk
Cheese or meat sandwich with whole wheat bread

Lunch
Mixed salad with either chicken, tuna, salmon, sausage, ham or beef.
Glass of milk

Supper (large meal)
Meat or fish dish
Potatoes, vegetables

Dessert based on fresh fruit
Beverage

Before Retiring to Bed
Glass of milk

What exactly are "repetitions" and "Sets"?

The word repetitions or "reps" is used to denote the number of "counts" you perform during a certain exercise. For example, if you perform 10 presses, then that would be ten reps. Do 12 "curls" and that would be 12 "reps" and so on. . .The term "sets" is one series of an exercise. For example, if you did ten squats and then stopped for a rest, that would be one "set" of ten reps. For the sake of convenience this is written 3 × 10 (three sets of ten reps). Five sets of eight reps would be written 5 × 8.

How much "rest" should one take between "sets"?

The amount of rest one should take between sets of an exercise varies. During your first few workouts (as you get stronger and more fit, you may rest for a couple of minutes or more between sets, but as your muscles and lungs get used to the exertion, you should constantly try to reduce the rest between sets, aiming for a minimum of 30 seconds or so. But don't be in too much of a rush to minimize your rest periods. Be patient, and gradually speed up your workout pace as your fitness, muscular strength and familiarity with the exercises increases.

How many sets and reps?

The idea is to tailor the severity of training to your needs, based upon age, sex, body type, your system, tolerance to stress, exercise, fatigue etc. Obviously, if your doctor feels that you are too old or unfit, or genetically unsuited to vigorous exercise, then this program is not for you. You have to go through life, or this program (or any course!) at your own individual pace.

One does 10 reps each set, but this varies according to mood and energy. Sometimes you may feel like doing 12 or even 15 repetitions. This is acceptable.

Beginners should keep to one set of each exercise for their first two weeks of workouts. After that, three sets may be performed of each movement. Advanced trainers may slowly graduate to five sets if they are so inclined, and sufficiently motivated.

What about warming up?

It is necessary to warm up the muscles before commencing, with a short run, some rope-jumping (skipping) or a few minutes on a jog-exerciser. In a similar vein, your workout is usually concluded with some non-weight movements such as sit-ups, twists or leg raises.

How do I do the exercises?

Don't just look at the illustrations. Read the description explaining how to perform each movement. You will then be 100% sure that you are performing the exercises in the correct manner. As a general rule, perform an exercise with a moderate steady movement, no bouncing, or swinging the weights. Just make sure that whatever you are doing, you do with an even, unstrained motion. A good tempo can be more beneficial than a very slow one. However, when you first learn a new exercise, you should perhaps perform it slowly, until you are exactly sure how it is executed. When you are thoroughly familiar with it, then you can speed up the tempo.

How much weight do I use?

This is entirely up to you. To begin with, it is far better to get into weight training by practicing with weight resistance you can easily handle for the stipulated number of repetitions. Suggested starting poundages are listed with each explanation of the movements. You may use slightly more or less depending on your current strength and condition. Never use so much weight on the barbell that the resistance causes you to strain, wobble and struggle to get it upwards. Every exercise should be done with a smooth rhythmic action.

MEN'S PROGRAM

Press Behind Neck (40 pound Barbell)

This works the shoulders and arms.

(i) Start with barbell held behind head as shown in Illustration A.

(ii) Press bar upwards (Illustration B) and return immediately to starting position.

(iii) Breathe "in" before starting to press upwards. Breathe "out" as the bar reaches the "arm lock" overhead position shown in Illustration B.

A

B

Straddle Lift (30 pound Barbell)

This exercise works the entire leg and hip area.

(i) Commence by holding the barbell as shown in Illustration C.

(ii) Lower slowly into attitude depicted in Illustration D. Keep back flat throughout movement.

(iii) Return to upright position and repeat.

(iv) Breathe "in" as you lower, breathe "out" as you return to upright position.

C

D

Bench Press (45 pound Barbell)

(i) You need a sturdy bench for this exercise. Approx 12″ width; by 4′.

(ii) Commence by holding a barbell (slightly wider than shoulder width grip) at arms length above head (Illus. E)

(iii) Lower slowly to upper chest; and immediately push up to original position.

(iv) Breathe "in" as weight is lowered to chest. Breathe "out" as bar is pushed up.

E

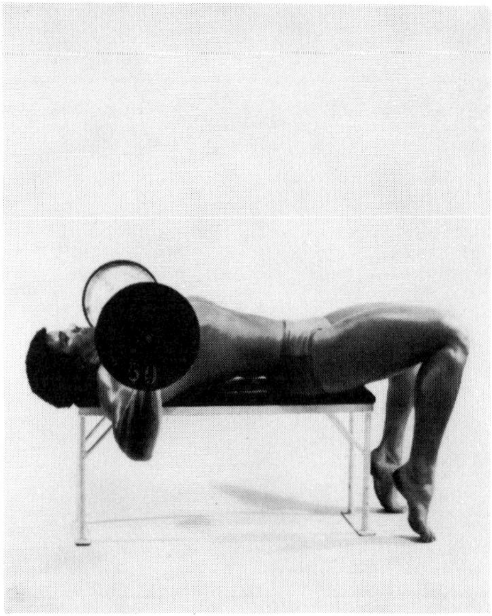

Single Arm Dumbell Rowing (30 pound Dumbell)
This works the back and arms.

(i) Illustration G shows the starting position for this exercise. If you wish, you may support the free hand with a chair or table.

(ii) Raise dumbell to position shown in the second picture; (Illus H).

(iii) Lower immediately to arms straight position and repeat.

(iv) Breathe "in" just before starting to raise the dumbell. Breathe "out" as the weight is being lowered.

G

H

Chin Behind Neck

This works the back and arms. Aids the development of a "V" shaped back in men. Most women would find this exercise too difficult to perform. (No weight)

(i) Adopt a "wide grip" position on an overhead horizontal bar. Illus. I.

(ii) Hold elbows backwards and pull up so that head is kept in front of the bar as shown in picture J.

(iii) Lower to starting position and repeat.

(iv) Breathe "in" before starting the pull upwards. Breathe "out" as you reach top position, (Illus. J).

I

J

Seated Barbell Curl (30 pound Barbell)
This is a specialized biceps exercise.

(i) Start in the seated position (on a strong bench or stool).
(ii) Hold the bar with "grip" approximately shoulder width as shown in position K.
(iii) Curl the bar upward until it is in position L. Lower and repeat.
(iv) Breathe in before starting. Breathe out as you slowly lower the bar.

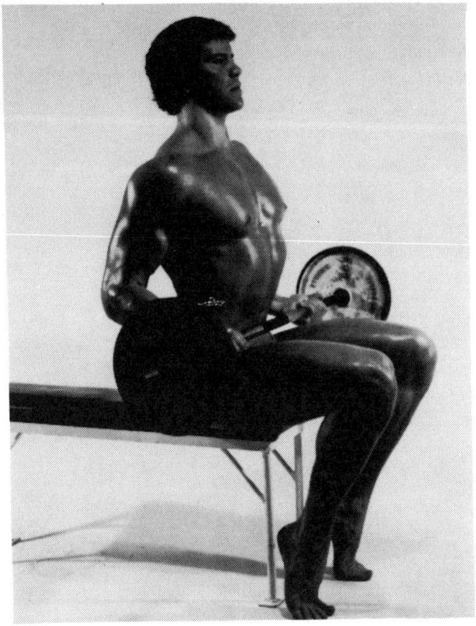

K

L

Incline Dumbell Curl (20 pound Dumbells)
Activates biceps and forearm muscles.

(i) Commence exercise as illustrated in picture M. An incline bench is needed for this movement.
(ii) Curl both dumbells simultaneously until weights touch shoulder area.
(iii) Lower and repeat, keeping head back against bench.
(iv) Breathe "in" before starting the "curl". Breathe "out" as you lower the dumbells.

M

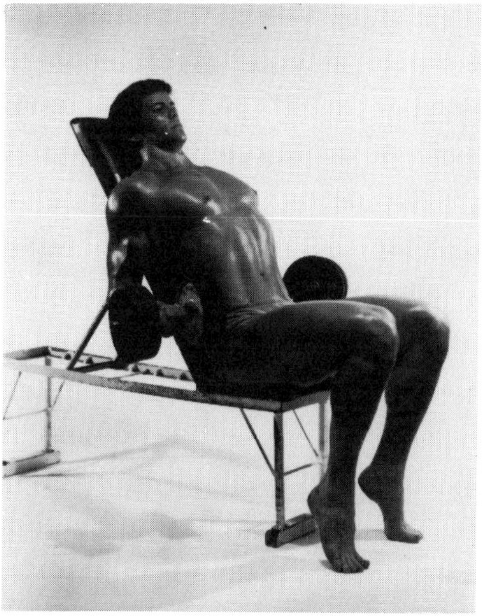

Triceps Stretch (25 pound Barbell)

Works the upper arms (triceps) and forearms.

(i) You need your flat bench again for this one.

(ii) Commence as shown in illustration O using light barbell.

(iii) Lower bar slowly to forehead and return to 'arms straight' position.

(iv) Breathe "in" as the weight is lowered; breathe "out" as arms straighten.

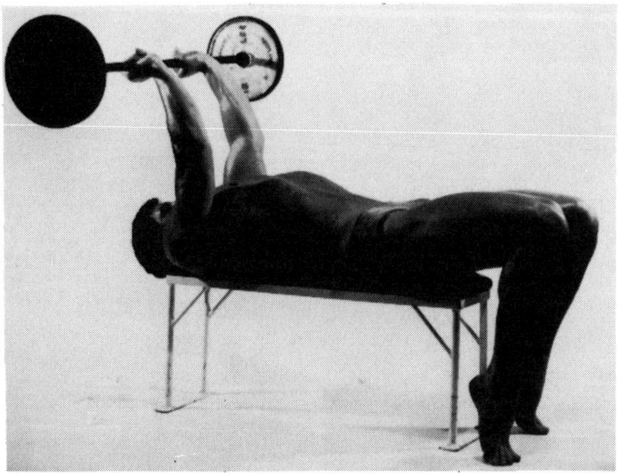

O

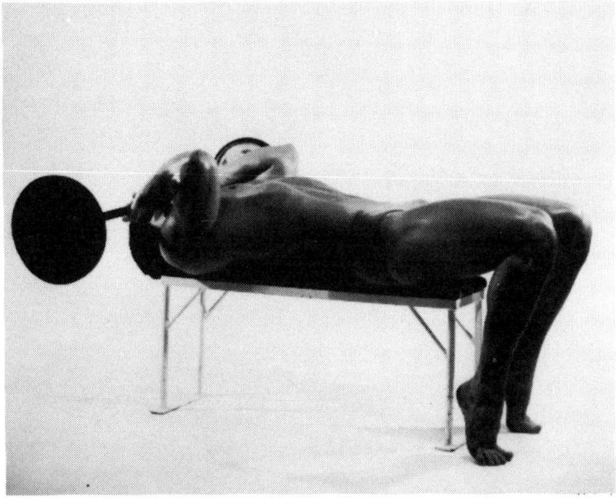

Incline Situps (No weight)
Works the waistline (abdominals)

(i) If you do not have an incline board, you may do this exercise on the floor. Get someone to hold your feet down if necessary.
(ii) Start, lying flat, arms placed either behind the head (Illus. R) or as shown in Illustration Q.
(iii) Raise body upwards into position R and lower slowly. Keep knees bent slightly.
(iv) Breathe "in" just before sitting up and "out" as the head nears the knees.

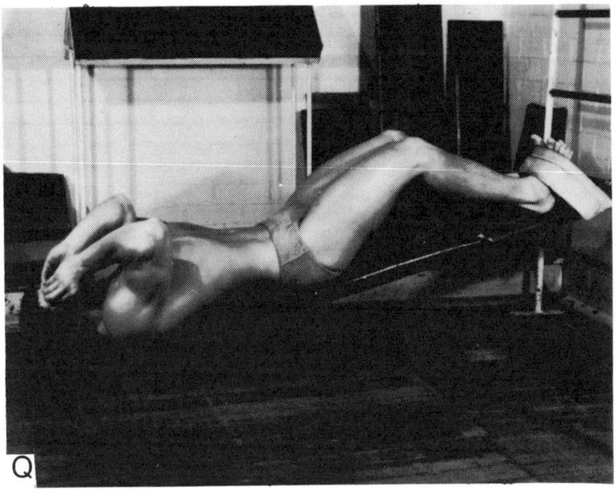
Q

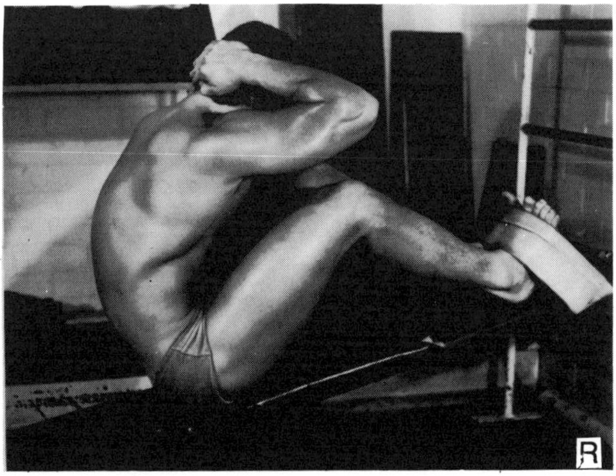
R

Side Twists (No weight)
Works entire waistline area.

(i) You need a bar, pole or broomstick for this one. Place it across your shoulders as illustrated.
(ii) Twist from side to side. Take care not to twist the hips too much.
(iii) Repeat slowly until abdominal muscles and waist area tire.
(iv) Breathe in and out with each twist, as desired.

WOMEN'S PROGRAM

Press Behind Neck (20 pound Barbell)
Shoulders, Neck, Back, Arms

(i) Start with a light barbell across the back of shoulders as shown in illustration A.
(ii) Slowly press weight to arms length (Illus. B) above head.
(iii) Lower and repeat 10-12 repetitions.
(iv) Breathe in before starting to press. Breathe out as arms straighten.

A

B

Upright Rowing (20 pound Barbell)
Shoulders, Back, Neck, Arms

(i) Begin with a light barbell held as shown in Illustration C.
(ii) Raise smoothly to position D, making sure that elbows are held high.
(iii) Lower and repeat 10-15 repetitions.
(iv) Breathe in before starting to raise arms. Breathe out as arms are lowered.

C

D

Straddle Lift (15 pound Barbell)

(i) The starting position E is commenced with a light barbell held between the legs, feet approximately 15 inches apart.

(ii) Lower steadily into position F, concentrating on maintaining upright balance.

(iii) Keeping back flat, raise up to original position and repeat 10-15 repetitions.

(iv) Breathe in as you go down. Breathe out as you return to upright position.

E

F

Bench Press (20 pound Barbell)
Chest, Shoulders, Arms.

(i) Lie on a flat bench with feet firmly on the ground, barbell held on upper chest as shown.
(ii) Press weight up evenly to arms straight (lockout) position shown.
(iii) Lower and repeat 8 repetitions.
(iv) Breathe out as you press the weight up. Breathe in as the bar is lowered.

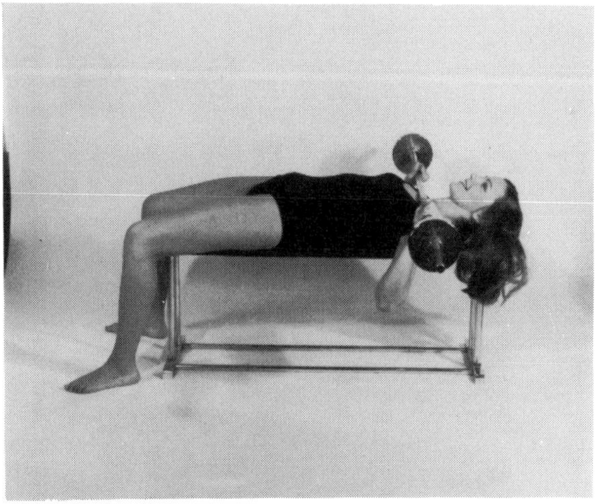

Inclined Bench Press (20 pound Barbell)
Upper chest, shoulders, arms.

(i) Commence with a light barbell held at the upper chest while lying back on an inclined bench (approximately 45° angle.)
(ii) Press weight up vertically to the arms straight position.
(iii) Lower to starting position and repeat 10 repetitions.
(iv) Breathe in before pushing bar up. Breathe out as the arms lock-out.

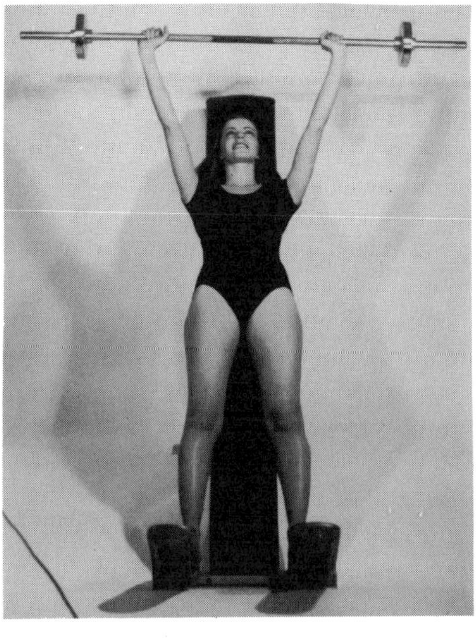

Single Arm Dumbell Row (15 pound dumbell)
Back, Arms, Shoulders.

(i) Illustration shows starting position with weight of upper body supported by free arm.
(ii) Raise weight to waist level, keeping elbow well back (light dumbell).
(iii) Lower and repeat for 10 repetitions.
(iv) Breathe in before starting to raise dumbell. Breathe out as the weight is lowered.

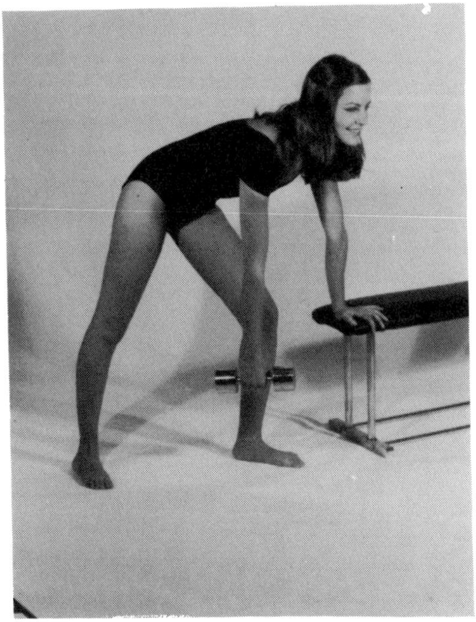

Incline Dumbell Press (5 pound Dumbell)

(i) Start with a pair of light dumbells as shown, while lying back on a 45° Inclined board.

(ii) Press dumbells simultaneously to the 'arms-straight' position.

(iii) Lower to starting position and repeat for 10 repetitions.

(iv) Breathe in before pressing dumbells up. Breathe out as the arms lock-out.

Seated Dumbell Curl (5 pound Dumbells)
Arms, Shoulders.

(i) Begin this movement again with two light dumbells while sitting on a chair, stool or bench (Illus. O).
(ii) Keep back straight as you curl the dumbells together to position shown.
(iii) Lower and repeat 12 repetitions.
(iv) Breathe in just before starting the "curl". Breathe out as the arms are again straightened.

Single Arm Dumbell Stretch (5 pound Dumbell)
Back of arms, shoulders.

(i) Another sitting exercise. Start with your upper arm pointing skyward as illustrated.
(ii) Keeping elbow near head, raise light dumbell to arms length overhead.
(iii) Lower and repeat 12 repetitions. Follow with the same number of repetitions with the other arm.
(iv) Breathe in as the dumbell is raised. Breathe out as it is lowered.

Regular Situp (No weight)
Overall midsection, waist.

(i) You may perform this on a bench as shown (Illus. S), or you may do it on the floor. The feet may be held down by a partner or placed under a bed to prevent the legs from raising.

(ii) With arms held behind the head raise trunk up as shown in Illustration T.

(iii) Lower and repeat 6-20 times, depending on strength and condition.

(iv) Breathe in before sitting up. Breathe out as you lower your body to flat position.

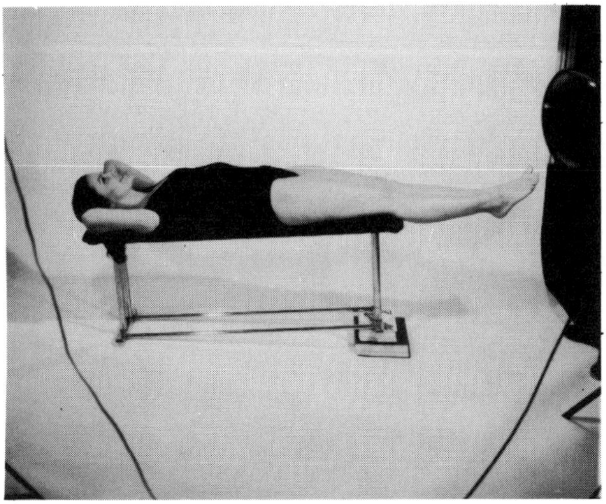

S

T

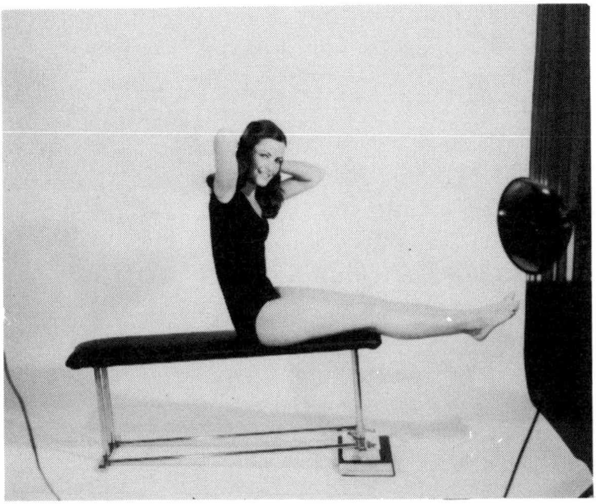

Beginners to progressive training need *not* perform *all* these exercises.

An ideal beginners schedule would be one set of:

(1) Upright Rowing (shoulders, back, neck, arms).
(2) Straddle lift (Thighs, hips, calves, lower back).
(3) Bench Press (Chest, shoulders, arms).
(4) Single arm rowing (Back, arms, shoulders).
(5) Regular sit-up (Waistline, mid-section).

After a month of the above schedule you may add some of the other exercises, according to the time you have available, your energy level and individual capacity for exercise.

Further severity can be added by performing each exercise twice; two sets of each instead of only one. For example, after performing 8 repetitions of your bench presses, you may rest a minute or two, and then perform a further set of 8 repetitions.

Never use a weight that prevents you from doing the exercises correctly, without strain. It is far better to use a barbell or dumbell that is too light rather than too heavy. There is no place for strain in this program. Best results come from sensible light training done on a regular basis, combined with a diet of wholesome natural foods, not overloaded with empty calories and heavy starches. Never make the mistake of thinking that exercise *alone* will shape you up. All progress is at least 70% dependent on correct diet and calorie allocation. My thoughts for your success are with you. . .always.

PART IV

YOUR DIET

Chapter 11

WE ARE WHAT WE EAT

Never was a quote so meaningful. We are indeed what we eat. Every morsel that passes between our lips is potentially destined to become part of our very being. Every limb, every muscle; our blood, hair, teeth, nails, even our skin is formed from the food we eat. All the more reason therefore to make sure that we ingest only the best foods. You wouldn't dream of putting bad gas in your car, yet the vast majority of people treat their own bodies with far less respect.

The food you eat is not just responsible for how much you weigh or how you look in a swim costume; it is a vital ingredient to your overall health and well-being. Everything from the sparkle in your eyes to the texture of your skin is dependent on what you eat.

It is your duty to feed yourself not only the correct amount of food but also the correct quality, not just next week or next month, but for the rest of your life!

It is a habit you can fall into as easily as you have fallen into your present eating regime. This book will show you how!

Reasons For Dieting

The main reason why most obese or overweight people want to lose weight is cosmetic. They simply want to *look* good. However, the most important reason could in fact be related to health.

If you are overweight and too fat you should diet to correct this abnormal condition. The main reason being that it should help to restore health, or at least prevent your health from deteriorating.

Some foods contribute to unhealthy conditions. There are foods which help some ailments and others which contribute to the worsening of illnesses. Because of the effects of foods on ailments like ulcers, inflamed bowels, high blood pressure, gallstones, heart disease, gout, diabetes, constipation, arthritis, malabsorption, pregnancy and nursing, kidney disease, etc., it is unreservedly recommended that before going on any diet an individual should have his or her state of health professionally assessed. This means that you should be examined by your physician. Should you be contemplating taking up any vigorous physical pursuits, you should also request a complete physical stress test. You need a competent examination and laboratory work-up to be sure that you are not one of these few people whose fatness is due to a hormone imbalance.

Overweight is a personal handicap. Dr. Louis Dublin, a statistician with Metropolitan Life Insurance Company says, "It often proves a handicap in the personal life of individuals. It can be a factor in employment, either because of the self-consciousness of the job-seeking overweight, or because of the preference employers may give to applicants who are of normal weight. It is also a handicap in social relationships and may give rise to emotional problems. The fat child is ridiculed by other children. He is, therefore, likely to shun them and seek satisfaction in sedentary recreation and in eating. The chances of marriage for the obese girl are less than for her thinner rival.

Whereas no one can claim that slimness guarantees automatic health right into old age, it is nevertheless true that obesity walks hand in hand with chronic disease and early death. Scientists have found that degenerative diseases are more common among the obese. Studies of former fatties who have reduced weight and kept fat off show that they tend to live longer than overweight people who remain fat.

A factual survey of 5 million insurance policy holders conducted by the Society of Actuaries in 1959 showed conclusively that earlier mortality is 50 percent greater in overweight policy holders than in those of normal weight. The studied data showed that the more overweight an individual was, the greater the chance of early death. As an example, men who were 10 percent overweight had 16 percent excess mortality over normal, with men 30 percent overweight there was 42 percent excess mortality. (Stat. Bull. Metropolitan Life Ins., Vol. 41, February 1960).

Accordingly, the insurance companies usually charge fat people higher premiums for the same coverage they give at lower premium to people of normal weights. These are scary statistics, but true. To ignore them would be wrong. There are numerous diseases which are linked with the obese condition which we will not mention here.

Losing your superfluous fat will not automatically bring about a perfect situation for you, but reducing weight can bring substantial benefits, of physical, psychological, social and economical well-being. Sensible dieting and maintenance of a trim body can help you look better, feel better and give you a greater chance of living a longer and happier life. "Don't dig your grave with your teeth," wrote Thomas C. Desmon, a former New York legislator. Aptly put.

You Are Not Alone

There are thousands of people who are overweight. You may see literally hundreds every day, wherever you go. You are not alone. I myself know the torment of being fat. In fact I have spent years on the diet "treadmill." I would discover a new diet system, give it a try, and be very conscientious in my efforts to remold my body.

But soon my enthusiasm would wane. I would lose it, perhaps after losing a few pounds or so, and ultimately give up my efforts in disgust. Consequently, I would gain back all my weight, and suffer the indignity of obesity all over again. Then I would try another system, then another. . .in fact, the whole cycle would be repeated year in and year out with monotonous regularity. Perhaps this all sounds familiar to you?

I finally decided once and for all to learn the real truth about losing weight. I consulted medical research papers on nutrition. I talked to professionals. I discovered the truth. Once I had made a full study, I applied the knowledge to my own case. Incredibly, for the first time in my life, I shed fat. In fact, as the weeks turned into months I lost every ounce of excess fat from my body. I had at last found the answer to gaining a new body, free from any surplus fat.

After years of defeat, the secret was in my hands. I formulated this method, which became famous as THERMODYNAMICS. Incorporate it with the movements illustrated later and you can shoot for the stars. Bodyshape will be your reward.

If you apply this principle to your own life, you too may join the sleek set. And why not? What is the sense of going through life with the weight of obesity on your body and mind. You deserve better, and with application you will get it!

What Usually Happens?

Because of the huge amounts of food we eat in the western world, unlike some eastern hemisphere dwellers who are relatively slim, and accordingly healthy, we have the largest percentage of fat and flabby people. America leads the way, with Canadians coming a close second, and the British fast catching up. The only way to counteract this overweight (brought about by excessive eating) is to eat less.

There are many diets on the market—your doctor can probably recommend one. There are group workshops like Weight Watchers, Diet Workshops, and T.O.P.S. (Take Off Pounds Sensibly) which offer sound advice.

Yet, there is one totally undeniable fact. LESS THAN ONE PERCENT OF ALL THOSE WHO START A DIET IN ORDER TO LOSE WEIGHT SUCCEED IN KEEPING THAT WEIGHT OFF!

Almost to a man(or woman) the diet is dropped and that old flab creeps back on. The reason, of course, is that one makes the mistake of thinking that once one has normalized body weight, that one can revert back to old eating habits. This is just not true. Once you have lost all your flab, you should never gain back more than a couple of pounds.

What I am telling you is that you will be on a "diet" for the rest of your life. Actually, you shouldn't think of it as a diet, but rather as an improved life-style of eating. You are to revolutionize your eating habits. In the process, you should be healthier, and stand a better chance of living to a vigorous old age.

A diet shouldn't be a harassing experience, it shouldn't be a bore. The food should be tasty, satisfying and nutritious. Because many recommended diets or eating plans do not conform to the above, we find that people cannot stay with them. They become bored or depressed (or both) and give up in disgust. . . .

Calorie Control Is The Only Way

Seemingly, one of the easiest things for most of us is to eat more food than our body needs, and, of course, to grow fat. True, there are some "natural" skinnies, people who have unusually high metabolisms, people who have very small bone structures, people who are forever in a worrying turmoil of non-stop mental and physical activity. However, the majority of us get fat with almost incredible ease, especially as the years go by. The unfair fact is that getting fat off is exceedingly more difficult than putting it on. Losing fat is also a relatively slow job. It seems to go on overnight and takes weeks to come off. With regard to the skinnies, we will deal with them later.

The acceptable way to become slim is to eat fewer calories. Possibly you suspected this, but surprisingly there are many advocates and followers of a multitude of different diet systems, based on unproven theoretical systems, which in turn do not advocate calorie counting. These systems invariably fall short in that they can be dangerous to health, or else they simply do not work.

When a body takes in as many calories as it burns up, this is known as thermodynamic balance. "Thermo" means heat, and "dynamic" refers to movement. This principle of recommended dieting is advocated by the A.M.A., Harvard University and the Public Health Service. (The North Americans have studied diet to a greater extent than their European counterparts.)

One way of simplifying thermodynamics is to look at it like a bank account. You start with a given amount of money in the bank (fat on your body). Making deposits is like eating, in that you add to the total in the bank. Writing a check can be regarded as exercise (walking, breathing, running). You subtract from the amount in the account. If your deposits equal your withdrawals, your balance (weight) will stay the same. If you spend as many calories as you eat, your body will stay the same. Burn more calories than you consume and your body will start losing weight. In practice, for example, if you eliminate just one pat of butter a day, you will not deposit some 3,780 calories each month! This represents one pound of fat 'burned off'. Twelve pounds a year. Eliminate 2 pats of butter per day and you're losing about one half a pound per week. This, of course, sounds great theoretically, but in practice it may well prove more difficult.

We should supply you with a caution here. A low calorie diet should include balanced nutrition—(good wholesome nutritional foods). To simply choose a food program of low caloried ingredients is not satisfactory. Foods should never be evaluated strictly on their calorie count. Dr. Jean Mayer of the Harvard School of Nutrition wrote, "A proper diet must provide all necessary nutrients in sufficient amounts, be palatable, easily available from the viewpoints of economics and convenience, and be limited in calories so as to produce the desired caloric deficit." (Jean Mayer, *Overweight*, Prentice-Hall).

What Is Good Nutrition?

Opinions vary as to exactly how much and what kind of foods we require for a balanced eating program. Speaking generally, one should select foods from the five main food groups:

1. Milk Group—milk, cheese, ice cream
2. Meat Group—beef, veal, lamb, pork, poultry, eggs, fish
3. Vegetable/Fruit Group
4. Bread/Grain Group—(Enriched or restored)
5. Fats/Oil Group—butter, margarine (usually only a small amount of these)

It may be advisable to supplement your diet with a multi-vitamin-mineral tablet each day, just to make sure that you are not missing out on any of these factors. But this is up to you.

Getting Back To Calories

You will have to do a little figuring—but it can be fun. You need to find out just how many calories you should eat a day.

As a quick guide you can say that a "cut" of 500 calories per day will cause you to lose one pound a week. This may not sound like much, but a pound a week is 50 pounds a year! A daily cut of 1000 calories will leave you 2 pounds lighter a week, and so on. This, of course, assumes that your physical activities won't change that much.

You should know how many calories you are presently consuming. Count them up as you go through your usual day. Don't miss any. Remember, if you have a quick snack, or a piece of chocolate, and don't record it on your daily calorie total, you are cheating no one but yourself. It is an accepted opinion that a person leading a moderately active life needs 15 calories per pound of body weight, every day.

Accordingly, look at the weight/height charts along with this program and find out how much you should weigh for your sex and age. These charts can never be perfect, but they give an *indication* of how heavy you should be.

Multiply your perfect weight by 15. The answer is the number of calories you need to ingest daily to maintain that weight.

As an example, if you are a man and you want to weigh 150 pounds (10 st. 10 lbs.) you should be eating 2250 calories a day just to keep at that weight. Substantially more daily calories will increase your weight-fewer will reduce it!

We suggest that you do not try to reduce your weight by more than 2 lbs. per week—(100 lbs. per year!) This is considered a safe rate at which to lose weight. You should not normally eat less than 1000-1200 calories per day, unless you do so under a doctor's close supervision.

It is difficult to say exactly how many calories you would be taking in every day, because of individual body chemistry and inherited traits. However, the table below is for your guidance in this area. Specific vital body functions are dependent upon vitamins, minerals and essential amino acids (building blocks of protein). Fats and carbohydrates play important roles. Needless to say, all nutrients depend on one another to carry on their tasks. They participate in complex interrelated systems. In other words, a shortage of one individual and essential dietary factor will impair the ability of others to function adequately. Alternatively, an over abundance of certain food stuffs such as saturated fat and refined carbohydrate (sugar) could well overtax the capacity of body mechanisms and interfere with vital metabolic processes. As we mentioned before, a well-

ACTIVITY AND CALORIC REQUIREMENTS

	INACTIVE (does nothing actively)	MILDLY ACTIVE (Rides to work, sits at work)	MEDIUM ACTIVE (Teacher, mother of small children)	ACTIVE (On the move most of the time)	VERY ACTIVE (Physical worker plus extra exercise)
Multiply weight by	12	14	16	18	20
Weight 94	1140	1330	1520	1710	1900
97	1176	1372	1568	1764	1960
100	1212	1414	1616	1818	2020
104	1260	1470	1680	1890	2100
109	1320	1540	1760	1980	2200
115	1380	1615	1840	2070	2300
121	1414	1680	1920	2160	2400
124	1500	1750	2000	2250	2500
129	1560	1820	2080	2340	2600
135	1620	1890	2160	2430	2700
141	1680	1960	2240	2520	2800
146	1740	2030	2320	2610	2900
150	1800	2100	2400	2700	3000
154	1860	2170	2480	2790	3100
160	1920	2240	2560	2880	3200
164	1980	2310	2640	2970	3300
174	2100	2450	2800	3150	3500
184	2220	2590	2960	3330	3700
194	2340	2730	3120	3510	3900
200	2400	2800	3200	2600	4000
209	2520	2940	3360	3780	4200
221	2640	3080	3520	3960	4400

balanced diet is one that provides all the necessary ingredients and adequate quantities to keep the complex machinery of the body functioning in the best possible way.

As a simple guide, the requirements of this body shape diet are:

Daily:

a) Milk or milk product.
b) A high protein ingredient with every meal.
c) Vegetables high in vitamin A (3-5 times a week).
d) Citrus fruits (vitamin C).
e) Whole grain breads (enriched breads/cereals).
f) Vegetable oils high in polyunsaturated fat.

Eggs are not recommended as a daily requirement (3-4 eggs a week are sufficient, more may not be beneficial). Children may have up to 7 a week. Poached or boiled eggs are advised, however you may add variety to your meals by taking your eggs in an egg salad, sandwich or by making a tasty omelette. Egg whites are not restricted at all since they contain no fat.

It could be said that virtually everyone needs milk everyday. Milk is man's best source of calcium. In order to maintain strong bones and teeth, we need sufficient calcium daily.

Children can drink up to a pint of milk a day, but adults should make sure that the milk they drink is fat reduced. In other words, skim off the cream or use a fat free milk powder. You may substitute a low fat yogurt for the usual lowfat milk if it is not available.

Cheese, in the form of cottage cheese or other low fat varieties are highly recommended. Stay away from the steady consumption of cream processed cheese, Camembert, cheddar or Swiss cheese. They are all high in fat.

Peanut butter is a food that is becoming popular in Europe and has enjoyed enormous acceptance, mainly for its taste, in North America.

However, in spite of its happy taste, (children love it), peanut butter is extremely nutritional, having a high vegetable-protein content, B vitamins and unsaturated fat. Peanut butter is mainly used as a sandwich spread.

Eating Suggestions:

Breakfast

Do not think that skipping breakfast is a good way of helping weight loss. If you miss out on this important meal you will find it doubly hard to eat sensibly at lunch time. In all probability you will not be in any mood to go easy at dinner time. Breakfast is an important meal which should consist of more than a cup of coffee. If you like conventional breakfasts, we have them. In fact, quite a few different breakfasts are listed. You may choose any of the following breakfasts, depending on your mood and hunger. If you wake up ravenous, then select a more substantial breakfast. As long as the calorie contents are listed and made part of your overall calorie allotment, you will not go wrong. Variety is most important, so don't hesitate to experiment with all the listed breakfasts.

Here are a few breakfast suggestions. Naturally, the amount you eat will depend on your caloric allotment. Artificial sweetners should be non-cyclamate.

1. 1 cup orange/grapefruit juice
   2 eggs (boiled or poached)
   1 rasher bacon
   tea/coffee (artificial sweetener)
2. 1 cup tomato juice/or V8 juice
   2 sausages
   1 large tomato
   tea/coffee (artificial sweetener)

3. Special K with milk (artificial sweetener)
   1 boiled egg
   tea/coffee

4. Strawberries and cream (artificial sweetener)
   1 round toast/jam
   tea/coffee (artificial sweetener)

5. Bowl of Special K and milk (artificial sweetener)
   2 ounces cottage cheese
   tea/coffee (artificial sweetener)

6. Hot Coffee Frappe
   Blend together:
   ⅓ cup skim milk powder
   ½ teaspoon instant coffee powder
   ½ teaspoon vanilla extract
   2 teaspoons liquid artificial sweetener
   ¾ cup hot water

7. Baked Grapefruit:
   Cut the fruit in half and slice into sections
   Remove membranes so as to allow as much space as possible
   Bake at 325F. for 15 minutes.
   1 egg, fried and sprinkled with seasoned salt
   toast
   tea/coffee (artificial sweetener)

8. Eggs with Herbs
   3 poached eggs flavored with herbs-dried or fresh
   1 cup orange juice
   1 round of buttered toast
   tea/coffee (artificial sweetener)

9. 1 cup apple juice
   2 sausages
   1 tomato
   tea/coffee (artificial sweetener)

10. ½ orange, diet sugar
    1 poached or boiled egg
    1 round toast, diet margarine
    marmalade
    lemon tea (artificial sweetener)

Lunch

Lunch is an easy meal to skip. But, like breakfast, it would be a mistake to do so. If you miss this important meal you may well give in to excessive snacking in the afternoon. And, once started, you may not be able to stop until the late evening. In other words, your diet will be ruined. You wouldn't expect your car to run without fuel. It is the same with your body. Going without lunch means an onset of hunger pangs later in the day. This may result in an overladen dinner plate later in the evening. There are many individuals who swear they never eat a thing all day long. They may be telling the truth, but, what they neglect to say is that they snack constantly from 7 p.m. until bedtime while watching T.V., and that's what makes them fat. Do you do this?

Many a mother has stated that she has no time to eat. The baby takes up all her time. Besides, "I don't care that much about food." However, if one was to study her eating habits for a few days, one may notice that while getting the baby's bottle out of the refrigerator, she also grabs several slices of luncheon meat, or some leftovers. While the baby was being held before going to sleep, she would perhaps dig into a bowl of salted nuts, sweets, candies or chocolate. Everytime her three-year-old asked for a biscuit, she put a few in her apron pocket so she could munch on them while going about her housework. Needless to say, this young mother was constantly upgrading her dress sizes, while at the same time believing that she did not over-eat.

It might well be in order for the reader to bear in mind that the most attractive curves and bodyline result from three square meals a day, with a gap of three to four hours between each eating session. Some days (especially when you have had a frugal breakfast) you will be absolutely ravenous. On these occasions you should take a substantial lunch, bearing in mind of course your overall calorie allotment for that day. Now that you are committed to this program, you *must* have lunch. You do not have the choice to "skip" it. Yes, lunch is mandatory, but, never have an "I'm famished" lunch when a smaller edition will suffice. Remember if you are not very hungry then do not eat very much. If you eat when not hungry the body will respond with actual demand for food, even when there is not a physiological need for it.

Many people have a definite problem with lunch because they have to eat at a restaurant. Accordingly, they have a limited menu to choose from, and, in many cases only so-called fattening foods are available. Soup, sandwiches, cake, buns, and biscuits are hardly acceptable ingredients for a would-be weight-loser. If you are unable to find a restaurant which can provide sensible nutrition for your particular needs, then, take definite steps to prepare your lunch before you go to work. It does not take much time to cut up a little cold beef, ham, tomato, lettuce, tuna, celery, chicken, apple, orange, etc. With a little thought you can prepare an ideal lunch and arrange it attractively in a handy sectionalized container (or any other airtight container for that matter). It is a good idea to cut your meat up into small pieces as opposed to preparing slices or large chunks. In this way you will fool yourself into thinking that you are eating more. Eat slowly and take only small amounts of anything. You will have reeducated your system to eating only small proportions. If you eat lunch at home then try some of the following tasty variations:

1. ½ cup Tuna fish (water packed)
   vinegar and/or lemon
   salad and diet dressing
   1 apple
   tea/coffee (artificial sweetener)

2. 1 cup consommé soup
   chopped cold beef
   2 medium sized tomatoes
   mixed fresh fruit salad
   tea/coffee (artificial sweetener)

3. 1 cup of chicken soup
   vegetable plate containing one cup wax beans
   ½ cup carrots, 1 cup broccoli
   4 saltines
   1 peach

4. 3 ounces cottage cheese
   1 teaspoon of Worcestershire sauce
   2 sticks of celery
   sliced orange with cream

5. Sliced or chopped chicken
   1 tomato, lettuce
   1 slice bread
   8-12 fresh grapes

6. Canned or smoked or fresh salmon
   pickles, lettuce
   1 apple

7. Green pepper
   cooked with minced meat and tomatoes
   grapefruit with artificial sweetener

8. Cold chicken breast
   small portion cheese and tomato
   mixed fresh fruit salad

9. Chopped ham
   1 slice hard boiled egg
   lettuce leaf

1 small tomato
1 cup cherries

10. Raw vegetable salad (tomatoes, celery, carrots, green pepper etc.).
    yogurt flavored with honey

11. Broth
    fresh dover sole
    slices (whole wheat) bread and diet margarine
    tea/coffee (artificial sweetener)

12. Cottage cheese omelette with stewed tomatoes
    1 apple
    tea/coffee (artificial sweetener)

13. Sardines with sliced hard boiled egg
    1 tangerine
    tea/coffee (artificial sweetener)

14. Shrimps with celery and tomatoes
    mayonnaise
    2 ounces cream

Dinner

Dinner is probably the most enjoyed meal of the day. Breakfast often causes nausea, especially when one is rushed and forced to bolt one's food. Lunch is often rushed by circumstances beyond our control. Dinner is different. It comes at the end of the work-day. It is the king of meals. I firmly believe it should receive due attention. Dinner in my opinion should be a multi-course meal, and, for full enjoyment, the greater the variety the better it comes. Dinner should be substantial. After all there is going to be a 10 or 12 hour gap until your next meal. A successful dinner evolves from variety and quality. It is true that many diet conscious people get into the habit of just eating steak and a lettuce leaf for dinner. Or, on special occasions, they may throw in a tomato to add a bit of color to the plate. However, if you will thrive best on variety at dinnertime, you will need to try something new. Here are a few varieties of dinner which may fit the bill. Again, amounts must fit in with your daily calorie allotment.

1. Consommé soup
   poached shellfish with tartar sauce or mayonnaise
   fresh melon
   coffee, cream and artificial sweetener

2. Clam broth
   duckling (roasted or broiled)
   fresh vegetables (carrots, peas)
   fresh fruit salad
   tea/coffee (artificial sweetener)

3. Gazpacho soup
   broiled filet of beef
   3 new potatoes
   tossed green salad with French dressing
   sliced apple and orange fruit cup
   tea/coffee (artificial sweetener)

4. ½ grapefruit
   roast veal, haricot beans
   fruit gelatin or jelly
   tea/coffee (artificial sweetener)

5. V8 vegetable juice
   roast lamb/mint sauce
   mashed potato
   melon
   tea/coffee (artificial sweetener)

7. Asparagus
   steak

new potatoes, tomato
fruit salad
tea/coffee (artificial sweetener)

8. Tossed green salad
   Italian or French dressing
   beef broth, slice dry bread
   shish kebab
   tangerine
   tea/coffee (artificial sweetener)

9. Prawn cocktail
   ½ melon
   gammon steak
   pineapple slice
   broccoli
   sliced peaches and apple salad
   tea/coffee (artificial sweetener)

10. Fish fingers
    sirloin, asparagus
    tomato
    black currants and slice apple

11. ½ avocado with prawns and vinegar (cider or wine vinegar preferably)
    braised kidneys
    1 potato
    runner beans
    rhubarb
    tea/coffee (artificial sweetener)

Now, for your guide in counting up your daily calorie intake, I have listed over 500 foods.

Many individuals want to know about the protein content of foods, or the fat content. Still others are interested in factors regarding nutritional ingredients such as calcium, iron, niacin, etc. Accordingly, we are listing an exhaustive amount of information which may help you understand the content of your foods.

Values are shown for protein, fat, fatty acids, carbohydrates, calcium, iron and five vitamins—Vitamin A, thiamin, riboflavin, niacin and ascorbic acid (Vitamin C). Calories are shown in the column headed "food energy." Water content is shown as an aid to identification of some food items.

The values shown are the amounts present in the edible part of the item, but if inedible parts are included in the description, e.g. cob of corn, both measure and weight include these parts. For meat, values are for meat as cooked, drained and without drippings. For some cuts two sets of values are given, meat including the fat, and meat from which the fat has been trimmed before eating.

Some foods have been fortified with minerals and vitamins by the manufacturer in accordance with regulations. If most brands in a category have been so fortified, this information has been included in the table, but if a produce has been fortified by only one or two manufacturers, the value for the unfortified product has been used. These food values have been identified in the table by appropriate symbols.

Values have been obtained from a variety of sources and may differ from values provided by any one source. If suitable values were not available, and it was believed that a measurable amount of a nutrient may be present, this was indicated in the table by dashes.

FOOD VALUES—NUTRIENTS AND CALORIES CHARTS

Abbreviations

tr.	trace	Tbsp.	tablespoon	oz.	ounce	g.	grams
%	percent	lb.	pound (16 ounces) = 453.6 grams	in.	inch	mg.	milligrams
c.	cup (8 fluid ounces)	oz.	ounce = 28.35 grams	"	inch	Cal.	Calories
—	no suitable value found but measurable amount may be present.			diam.	diameter	I.U.	International Units

	Food	Measure	Weight	Moisture	Food Energy	Protein	Fat	Fatty Acids: Saturated (Total)	Fatty Acids: Unsaturated: Oleic	Fatty Acids: Unsaturated: Lin-Oleic	Carbohydrate	Calcium	Iron	Vitamin A Value	Thiamine	Riboflavin	Niacin	Ascorbic Acid
			g.	%	Cal	g.	g.	g.	g.	g.	g.	mg.	mg.	I.U.	mg.	mg.	mg.	mg.
	MILK, CHEESE, CREAM, RELATED PRODUCTS																	
	Milk, fluid:																	
1	Whole, 3.5% fat	1 cup	244	87	160	9	9	5	3	tr.	12	288	0.1	350	0.07	0.41	0.2	2
2	Non fat (skim)	1 cup	245	90	90	9	tr.	—	—	—	13	298	0.1	10[1]	0.10	0.44	0.2	2
3	Partially skimmed, 2%	1 cup	245	87	123	9	5	3	2	tr.	12	294	0.1	172[1]	0.10	0.44	0.2	2
4	Buttermilk (from skim milk)	1 cup	245	90	90	9	tr.	—	—	—	13	298	0.1	10	0.09	0.44	0.2	2
	Milk, processed:																	
5	Evaporated, canned, unsweetened	1 cup	252	74	345	18	20	11	7	1	24	635	0.3	820	0.10	0.84	0.5	32*
6	Condensed, canned, sweetened	1 cup	306	27	980	25	27	15	9	1	166	802	0.3	1090	0.23	1.17	0.5	3
7	Dry, skim, instant (1⅓ c. needed for reconstitution to 32 ounces)	1 cup	68	4	245	24	tr.	—	—	—	35	879	0.4	20[1]	0.24	1.21	0.6	5
8	Dry, whole	1 Tbsp	6	2	32	2	2	1	1	tr.	2	59	tr.	70	0.02	0.09	tr.	tr.

	Milk Beverages:																	
9	Cocoa (made with whole milk)	1 cup	250	79	245	10	12	7	4	tr.	27	295	1.0	400	0.10	0.45	0.5	2
10	Chocolate drink (partially skimmed milk)	1 cup	250	83	190	8	6	3	2	tr.	27	270	0.5	210	0.10	0.40	0.3	2
11	Instant Breakfast (made with whole milk)	1 cup	298	—	304	18	9	5	3	tr.	39	544	4.6	1970	0.75	1.65	6.3	23
12	Instant Breakfast, powder	1 envelope	37	—	146	9	1	—	—	—	25	233	5.0	1600	0.60	1.00	6.0	20
13	Malted milk—beverage	1 cup	270	83	280	13	12	—	—	—	32	364	0.8	670	0.17	0.56	0.2	2
14	Ovaltine (with whole milk)	1 cup	259	83	221	11	10	6	4	tr.	22	373	4.0	1070	0.39	0.67	2.3	10
	Milk Desserts:																	
15	Cornstarch Pudding—cooked	½ cup	124	38	137	5	5	3	2	tr.	20	145	0.1	195	0.04	0.20	0.1	1
16	Cornstarch Pudding—instant	½ cup	157	—	182	6	5	3	2	tr.	32	150	0.5	180	0.05	0.23	0.1	1
17	Custard—baked	½ cup	124	38	142	7	7	3	3	tr.	14	139	0.5	435	0.05	0.23	0.1	tr.
18	Rice pudding	½ cup	97	—	141	3	3	—	—	—	26	95	0.4	110	0.03	0.13	0.2	tr.
19	Tapioca pudding (minute)	½ cup	105	—	133	5	5	—	—	—	17	105	0.5	310	0.05	0.19	0.1	1
	Ice Cream:																	
20	Regular (approx. 10% fat)	1 cup	133	63	255	6	14	8	5	tr.	28	194	0.1	590	0.05	0.28	0.1	1
21	Rich (approx. 16% fat) ¼ brick = ½ cup	1 cup	148	63	330	4	24	13	8	1	27	115	tr.	980	0.03	0.16	0.1	1
22	Ice Milk, soft serve	1 cup	175	67	265	8	9	5	3	tr.	39	273	0.2	370	0.09	0.39	0.2	2
23	Ice cream bar	1 bar	60	—	144	3	8	—	—	—	16	98	0	80	0.04	0.14	0.1	0
24	Sherbet, lemon	1 cup	130	67	223	5	5	—	—	—	46	147	0.1	200	0.06	0.22	0.1	8
	Yoghurt:																	
25	Made from partially skimmed milk, plain	6 oz.	185	89	112	9	3	2	1	tr.	13	310	0.1	130	0.08	0.45	0.2	2
26	Made from partially skimmed milk, fruit flavoured (average)[7]	6 oz.	185	89	170	8	3	2	1	tr.	30	230	0.1	100	0.07	0.32	0.2	2

1. Value applies to unfortified product. Refer to label for information concerning addition of vitamins.
7. Calories vary according to flavour. Average values of several flavours were used.
* Added by manufacturer in accordance with Food and Drug Regulations.

	Food	Measure	Weight	Moisture	Food Energy	Protein	Fat	Fatty Acids: Saturated (Total)	Fatty Acids: Unsaturated: Oleic	Fatty Acids: Unsaturated: Lin-Oleic	Carbohydrate	Calcium	Iron	Vitamin A Value	Thiamine	Riboflavin	Niacin	Ascorbic Acid
			g.	%	Cal	g.	g.	g.	g.	g.	g.	mg.	mg.	I.U.	mg.	mg.	mg.	mg.
	MILK, CHEESE, CREAM, RELATED PRODUCTS (Continued)																	
	Cheese:																	
27	Blue	1 oz.	28	40	105	6	9	5	3	tr.	1	89	0.1	350	0.01	0.17	0.3	0
28	Camembert	1 oz.	28	52	84	5	5	3	2	tr.	1	29	0.1	280	0.01	0.21	0.2	0
29	Cheddar (1″ cube = 17 gms.)	1 oz.	28	37	116	7	8	5	3	tr.	tr.	211	0.3	360	tr.	0.13	tr.	0
30	Cheddar grated	1 Tbsp.	7	37	30	2	2	1	1	tr.	tr.	52	0.1	90	tr.	0.03	tr.	0
31	Cheddar processed	1 oz.	28	40	105	7	9	5	3	tr.	tr.	219	0.3	350	tr.	0.12	tr.	0
32	Cottage creamed—(4% fat)	1 cup	225	79	240	31	9	5	3	tr.	7	212	0.7	380	0.07	0.56	0.2	0
33	Cottage not creamed	1 cup	200	79	170	34	1	4	tr.	tr.	5	180	0.8	20	0.06	0.56	0.2	0
34	Cream	1 oz., 2 Tbsp.	28	51	105	2	11	6	4	tr.	1	18	0.1	440	tr.	0.07	tr.	0
35	Parmesan—grated	1 Tbsp.	7	—	28	2	2	—	—	—	tr.	80	tr.	80	tr.	0.05	tr.	0
36	Pasteurized, processed, cheese spread	1 oz., 2 Tbsp.	28	43	90	6	7	4	2	tr.	2	162	0.2	280	0.01	0.16	tr.	0
37	Swiss—natural	1 oz.	28	39	105	8	8	4	3	tr.	1	262	0.3	320	tr.	0.11	tr.	0
38	Swiss—processed—domestic	1 oz.	28	40	100	8	8	4	3	tr.	1	251	0.3	310	tr.	0.11	tr.	0
39	Swiss—processed—gruyere	1 oz.	28	40	115	8	9	5	3	tr.	1	308	0.3	560	0	0.14	0.1	0
	Cream:																	
40	Cereal Cream	1 cup	242	80	293	7	23	13	7	1	10	250	0.3	960	0.09	0.36	0.2	3
41	Cereal Cream	1 Tbsp.	15	80	18	tr.	1	1	tr.	tr.	1	16	tr.	60	tr.	0.02	tr.	tr.
42	Table cream (18% fat)	1 cup	240	72	505	7	49	27	16	1	10	245	0.1	2020	0.07	0.36	0.1	2
43	Table cream (18% fat)	1 Tbsp.	15	72	30	1	3	2	1	tr.	1	15	tr.	130	tr.	0.02	tr.	tr.
44	Whipping cream (35% fat) (unwhipped)	1 cup	239	57	691	5	73	41	25	2	8	184	0	3000	0.05	0.30	0.2	3
45	Whipping cream (35% fat) (unwhipped)	1 Tbsp.	15	57	43	tr.	5	3	2	tr.	tr.	11	0	190	tr.	0.02	tr.	tr.
46	Sour cream (10-18% fat)	1 cup	230	72	485	7	47	26	16	1	10	235	0.1	1930	0.07	0.35	0.1	2
47	Sour cream (10-18% fat)	1 Tbsp.	12	72	25	tr.	2	1	1	tr.	1	12	tr.	100	tr.	0.02	tr.	tr.
48	Whipped cream (pressurized) (18-26% fat)	1 Tbsp.	3	62	10	tr.	1	tr.	tr.	tr.	tr.	3	—	30	—	tr.	—	—

	Imitation Cream Products (vegetable fat)																	
	Creamers:																	
49	Powdered	1 Tsp.	2	2	10	tr.	1	tr.	tr.	0	1	1	tr.	tr.	—	—	—	—
50	Liquid (frozen)	1 Tbsp.	15	77	20	tr.	2	1	tr.	0	2	2	—	10	0	0	—	—
	Toppings:																	
51	Whipped—pressurized	1 Tbsp.	4	61	10	tr.	1	1	tr.	0	tr.	tr.	—	20	—	0	—	—
52	Powdered—made with whole milk	1 Tbsp.	6	58	14	0	1	tr.	tr.	tr.	1	5	0	10	tr.	tr.	tr.	0
	EGGS																	
	Eggs, large, (24 ounces per dozen):																	
	Raw or cooked in shell:																	
53	Whole, without shell	1 egg	50	74	80	6	6	2	3	tr.	tr.	27	1.1	590	0.05	0.15	tr.	0
54	White of egg	1 white	33	88	15	4	tr.	—	—	—	tr.	3	tr.	0	tr.	0.09	tr.	0
55	Yolk of egg	1 yolk	17	51	60	3	5	2	2	tr.	tr.	24	0.9	580	0.04	0.07	tr.	0
56	Scrambled with milk and fat	1 egg	64	72	110	7	8	3	3	tr.	1	51	1.1	690	0.05	0.18	tr.	0
57	Fried	1 egg	55	—	113	6	10	4	4	tr.	—	28	1.1	740	0.05	0.15	0	0
	MEAT, POULTRY, FISH, SHELLFISH; RELATED PRODUCTS																	
	Beef cooked:																	
	Ground beef, broiled:																	
58	Lean	3 oz.	85	60	185	23	10	5	4	tr.	0	10	3.0	20	0.08	0.20	5.1	—
59	Regular	3 oz.	85	54	245	21	17	8	8	tr.	0	9	2.7	30	0.07	0.18	4.6	—
	Roast, oven, no liquid:																	
	Relatively fat, such as rib:																	
60	Lean and fat	3 oz.	85	40	375	17	34	16	15	1	0	8	2.2	70	0.05	0.13	3.1	—
61	Lean only	1.8 oz.	51	57	125	14	7	3	3	tr.	0	6	1.8	10	0.04	0.11	2.6	—
	Relatively lean, such as round:																	
62	Lean and fat	3 oz.	85	62	165	25	7	3	3	tr.	0	11	3.2	10	0.06	0.19	4.5	—
63	Lean only	2.7 oz.	78	65	125	24	3	1	1	tr.	0	10	3.0	tr.	0.06	0.18	4.3	—
	Steak, broiled																	
	Relatively fat, such as sirloin:																	
64	Lean and fat	3 oz.	85	44	330	20	27	13	12	1	0	9	2.5	50	0.05	0.16	4.0	—
65	Lean only	2.0 oz.	56	59	115	18	4	2	2	tr.	0	7	2.2	10	0.05	0.14	3.6	—

	Food	Measure	Weight	Moisture	Food Energy	Protein	Fat	Fatty Acids: Saturated (Total)	Fatty Acids: Unsaturated: Oleic	Fatty Acids: Unsaturated: Lin-Oleic	Carbohydrate	Calcium	Iron	Vitamin A Value	Thiamine	Riboflavin	Niacin	Ascorbic Acid
			g.	%	Cal	g.	g.	g.	g.	g.	g.	mg.	mg.	I.U.	mg.	mg.	mg.	mg.
	MEAT, POULTRY, FISH, SHELLFISH; RELATED PRODUCTS (Continued)																	
	Beef Cooked: (Continued)																	
	Relatively lean, such as round:																	
66	Lean and fat	3 oz.	85	55	220	24	13	6	6	tr.	0	10	3.0	20	0.07	0.19	4.8	—
67	Lean only	2.4 oz.	68	61	130	21	4	2	2	tr.	0	9	2.5	10	0.06	0.16	4.1	—
	Stewing beef or pot roast, braised:																	
68	Lean and fat	3 oz.	85	53	245	23	16	8	7	tr.	0	10	2.9	30	0.04	0.18	3.5	—
69	Lean only	2.5 oz.	72	62	140	22	5	2	2	tr.	0	10	2.7	10	0.04	0.16	3.3	—
	Beef, canned:																	
70	Corned beef	3 oz.	85	59	185	22	10	5	4	tr.	0	17	3.7	20	0.01	0.20	2.9	—
71	Corned beef hash	3 oz.	85	67	155	7	10	5	4	tr.	9	11	1.7	—	0.01	0.08	1.8	—
	Pork, cured, cooked:																	
72	Bacon, back, sliced	1 slice	21	54	65	6	4	1	2	tr.	3	4	—	0	0.18	0.03	1.1	0
73	Bacon, side (20 slices per lb., raw) fried crisp	2 slices	15	8	90	5	8	3	4	1	1	2	0.5	0	0.08	0.05	0.8	0
74	Ham, lean and fat, roasted	3 oz.	85	54	245	18	19	7	8	2	0	8	2.2	0	0.40	0.16	3.1	—
75	Ham, boiled, sliced	2 oz.	57	59	135	11	10	4	4	1	0	6	1.6	0	0.25	0.09	1.5	—
76	Luncheon meat, canned, spiced or unspiced	2 oz.	57	55	165	8	14	5	6	1	1	5	1.2	0	0.18	0.12	1.6	—
	Pork,[2] fresh, cooked:																	
77	Chop, thick, with bone (4 per lb.)	1 chop	98	42	260	16	21	8	9	2	0	8	2.2	0	0.63	0.18	3.8	—
78	Chop, lean and fat	2.3 oz.	66	42	260	16	21	8	9	2	0	8	2.2	0	0.63	0.18	3.8	—
79	Chop, lean only	1.7 oz.	48	53	130	15	7	2	3	1	0	7	1.9	0	0.54	0.16	3.3	—
	Cuts, simmered:																	
80	Cuts, lean and fat	3 oz.	85	46	320	20	26	9	11	2	0	8	2.5	0	0.46	0.21	4.1	—
81	Cuts, lean only	2.2 oz.	63	60	135	18	6	2	3	1	0	8	2.3	0	0.42	0.19	3.7	—
	Roast, oven cooked, no liquid:																	
82	Lean and fat	3 oz.	85	46	310	21	24	9	10	2	0	9	2.7	0	0.78	0.22	4.7	—

83	Lean only	2.4 oz.	68	55	175	20	10	3	4	1	0	9	2.6	0	0.73	0.21	4.4	—
84	Salt pork (3″ x 1½″ x ¼″)	2 pieces	50	—	341	6	35	—	—	—	—	4	0.8	0	0.14	0.05	1.0	—
85	Spareribs—1¾″ pieces	6 pieces	45	0	123	8	10	4	4	1	0	4	1.1	0	0.20	0.07	1.4	0
	Sausage:																	
86	Bologna, slice 3″ diam. by ⅛″	2 slices	26	56	80	3	7	—	—	—	tr.	2	0.5	—	0.04	0.06	0.7	—
87	Braunschweiger, slice 2″ diam. by ¼″	2 slices	20	53	65	3	5	—	—	—	tr.	2	1.2	1310	0.03	0.29	1.6	—
88	Pork links, cooked (16 links per pound, raw)	2 links	26	35	125	5	11	4	5	1	tr.	2	0.6	0	0.21	0.09	1.0	—
89	Salami, dry type	1 oz.	28	30	130	7	11	—	—	—	tr.	4	1.0	—	0.10	0.07	1.5	—
90	Salami, cooked	1 oz.	28	51	90	5	7	—	—	—	tr.	3	0.7	—	0.07	0.07	1.2	—
91	Wieners, heated (8 per pound)	1 wiener	56	57	170	7	15	—	—	—	1	3	0.8	—	0.08	0.11	1.4	—
	Veal and Lamb:																	
	Lamb,[2] cooked:																	
	Chop, thick with bone, broiled, 1 chop:	4.8 oz.	137	47	400	25	33	18	12	1	0	10	1.5	—	0.14	0.25	5.6	—
92	Lean and fat	4.0 oz.	112															
93	Lean only	2.6 oz.	74	62	140	21	6	3	2	tr.	0	9	1.5	—	0.11	0.20	4.5	—
	Leg, roasted:																	
94	Lean and fat	3 oz.	85	54	235	22	16	9	6	tr.	0	9	1.4	—	0.13	0.23	4.7	—
95	Lean only	2.5 oz.	71	62	130	20	5	3	2	tr.	0	9	1.4	—	0.12	0.21	4.4	—
	Shoulder, roasted:																	
96	Lean and fat	3 oz.	85	50	285	18	23	13	8	1	0	9	1.0	—	0.11	0.20	4.0	—
97	Lean only	2.3 oz.	64	61	130	17	6	3	2	tr.	0	8	1.0	—	0.10	0.18	3.7	—
	Veal, cooked, bone removed:																	
98	Cutlet or chop without bone	3 oz.	85	60	185	23	9	5	4	tr.	—	9	2.7	—	0.06	0.21	4.6	—
99	Roast	3 oz.	85	55	230	23	14	7	6	tr.	0	10	2.9	—	0.11	0.26	6.6	—
	Liver:																	
100	Beef liver, fried	2 oz.	57	57	130	15	6	—	—	—	3	6	5.0	30280	0.15	2.37	9.4	15
101	Calves liver, fried (3″ × 2¼″ × ⅜″)	2 slices	72	52	147	16	7	—	—	—	3	5	9.0	19130	0.13	2.38	11.7	26
102	Chicken liver, fried:	2 livers	60	65	148	18	7	—	—	—	2	—	6.0	25760	0.11	1.77	9.4	8
103	Pork liver, fried (3″ × 2¼″ × ⅜″)	2 slices	74	54	170	18	7	—	—	—	8	10	15.6	12070	0.25	2.30	12.4	10

2. Outer layer of fat on cut trimmed to approx. ½ inch of the lean.

	Food	Measure	Weight	Moisture	Food Energy	Protein	Fat	Fatty Acids: Saturated (Total)	Fatty Acids: Unsaturated: Oleic	Fatty Acids: Unsaturated: Lin-Oleic	Carbohydrate	Calcium	Iron	Vitamin A Value	Thiamine	Riboflavin	Niacin	Ascorbic Acid
			g.	%	Cal	g.	g.	g.	g.	g.	g.	mg.	mg.	I.U.	mg.	mg.	mg.	mg.
	MEAT, POULTRY, FISH, SHELLFISH; RELATED PRODUCTS (Continued)																	
	Poultry:																	
	Chicken cooked																	
	Breast, fried (½ breast):																	
104	with bone	3.3 oz.	94	58	155	25	5	1	2	1	1	9	1.3	70	0.04	0.17	11.2	—
105	flesh and skin only	2.7 oz.	76	58	155	25	5	1	2	1	1	9	1.3	70	0.04	0.17	11.2	—
	Drumstick, fried:																	
106	with bone	2.1 oz.	59	55	90	12	4	1	2	1	tr.	6	0.9	50	0.03	0.15	2.7	—
107	flesh and skin only	1.3 oz.	38	55	90	12	4	1	2	1	tr.	6	0.9	50	0.03	0.15	2.7	—
108	Meat only (1 c. diced = 5⅓ oz.)	3 oz.	85	71	115	20	3	1	1	1	0	8	1.4	80	0.05	0.16	7.4	—
109	Chicken, canned, no bone	3 oz.	85	65	170	18	10	3	4	2	0	18	1.3	200	0.03	0.11	3.7	3
110	Turkey, roast, meat only	3 oz.	85	56	160	25	6	—	—	—	0	24	5.0	10	0.06	0.14	5.8	0
	Variety Meats:																	
111	Beef Heart (braised)	3 oz.	85	61	160	27	5	—	—	—	1	5	5.0	20	0.21	1.04	6.5	1
112	Beef Kidney, cooked (3¼″ × 2½″ × ¼″)	3 pieces	93	53	169	18	10	—	—	—	1	11	9.5	1240	0.18	1.99	3.8	0
113	Beef Tongue, braised	3 oz.	85	61	210	18	14	—	—	—	tr.	6	1.9	—	0.04	0.25	3.0	—
114	Pork Kidney, cooked	3½ oz.	100	55	114	16	5	—	—	—	1	11	8.0	130	0.58	0.17	9.8	13
115	Rabbit	3½ oz.	100	60	177	31	5	—	—	—	0	—	—	—	0.11	0.15	7.0	0
116	Sweetbreads	3½ oz.	100	63	184	15	13	—	—	—	0	10	1.2	20	0.04	0.04	3.1	44
	Fish and Shellfish:																	
117	Anchovy (fillet)	3 fillets	12	59	21	2	1	—	—	—	tr.	20	0	0	0	0	0	0
118	Clams, canned, solid and liquid	3 oz.	85	86	45	7	1	—	—	—	2	47	3.5	—	0.01	0.09	0.9	—
119	Cod, fried in butter	4 oz.	95	65	162	26	5	2	1	tr.	—	29	0.9	170	0.08	0.10	2.8	—
120	Crab, canned	3 oz.	85	77	85	15	2	—	—	—	1	38	0.7	—	0.07	0.07	1.6	—
121	Fish sticks, breaded, frozen (3.8″ × 1″ × ½″)	8 oz. pkg.	227	66	400	38	20	5	4	10	15	25	0.9	—	0.09	0.16	3.6	—

122	Haddock, fried, breaded	3 oz.	85	66	140	17	5	1	3	tr.	5	34	1.0	—	0.03	0.06	2.7	2
123	Halibut, grilled with butter	3 oz.	85	67	146	21	6	—	—	—	0	14	0.7	580	0.04	0.06	7.1	—
124	Herring, grilled	1 herring	85	63	217	21	14	—	—	—	—	—	1.2	130	0.14	0.15	3.3	—
125	Lobster, boiled + 2 Tbsp butter	1 lobster	334	77	308	20	25	12	8	tr.	1	80	0.7	920	0.11	0.06	2.3	0
126	Lobster, canned	3 oz.	85	77	150	31	2	—	—	—	—	110	1.4	—	0.06	0.12	3.8	—
127	Mackerel, cooked	3 oz.	85	62	200	19	13	—	—	—	0	5	1.0	450	0.13	0.23	6.5	—
128	Ocean perch, breaded, fried	3 oz.	85	59	195	16	11	—	—	—	6	28	1.1	—	0.08	0.09	1.5	—
129	Oysters, raw, meat only, medium size (13-14)	1 cup	240	85	160	20	4	—	—	—	8	226	13.2	740	0.33	0.43	6.0	—
130	Pike	3½ oz.	100	80	84	19	1	—	—	—	0	62	0.7	900	0.03	0.09	—	—
131	Salmon, canned	3 oz.	85	71	120	17	5	1	1	tr.	0	167[4]	0.7	60	0.03	0.16	6.8	—
132	Salmon, fresh, fried in butter	3 oz.	85	71	155	23	6	1	1	tr.	0	—	1.0	140	0.14	0.05	6.2	—
133	Sardines, canned in oil, solids only	3 oz.	85	62	175	20	9	—	—	—	0	372	2.5	190	0.02	0.17	4.6	—
134	Scallops, cooked	6 scallops	100	73	112	23	1	—	—	—	—	115	3.0	—	—	—	—	—
135	Shrimp—raw—20 small	⅔ cup	100	70	91	19	1	—	—	—	2	63	1.6	0	0.02	0.03	3.2	—
136	—fried—1 large 15 gr.	6 (approx.)	100	70	225	20	11	—	—	—	10	72	2.0	0	0.04	0.08	2.7	—
137	—canned, meat only	⅔ cup	85	70	100	21	1	—	—	—	1	98	2.6	50	0.01	0.03	1.5	—
138	Sole—fillet, in butter	3 oz.	85	58	172	26	7	3	2	tr.	0	20	1.2	—	0.06	0.07	2.0	—
139	Trout—raw	3½ oz.	100	78	167	18	10	—	—	—	0	20	1.0	—	0.09	0.20	3.5	—
140	Tuna—canned, solids only	3 oz.	85	61	170	24	7	2	1	1	0	7	1.6	70	0.04	0.10	10.1	—
	Meat, Poultry and Fish Combination Dishes:																	
141	Beef and Vegetable Stew	1 cup	235	82	210	15	10	5	4	tr.	15	28	2.8	2310	0.13	0.17	4.4	15
142	Beef pot pie baked, 4¼″ diam., weight before baking 8 ozs.	1 pie	227	63	560	23	33	9	20	2	43	32	4.1	1860	0.25	0.27	4.5	7
143	Cabbage rolls with meat	2 rolls	206	—	261	9	19	7	7	4	13	66	2.1	480	0.12	0.13	2.2	52
	Chili con carne, canned																	
144	with beans	1 cup	250	72	335	19	15	7	7	tr.	30	80	4.2	150	0.08	0.18	3.2	—
145	without beans	1 cup	255	67	510	26	38	18	17	1	15	97	3.6	380	0.05	0.31	5.6	—
146	Fish cake	¾ cup	134	53	166	18	7	2	2	tr.	6	179	0.9	140	0.07	0.19	7.3	5
147	Fish stew	1 cup	225	82	157	19	4	2	1	—	10	32	1.1	160	0.10	0.09	3.7	11
148	Irish stew	1 cup	200	82	280	23	16	9	6	—	10	17	1.8	10	0.19	0.25	5.4	11
149	Meat Loaf (4″ × 3″ × ⅜″)	1 slice	70	64	264	10	19	—	—	—	11	26	1.7	50	0.12	0.11	2.0	—
150	Poultry Pot pie, baked, 4¼″ diam., weight before baking 8 ozs.	1 pie	227	63	535	23	31	10	15	3	42	68	3.0	3020	0.25	0.26	4.1	5
151	Spaghetti sauce, meat and tomato	¼ cup	66	—	64	3	3	—	—	—	5	8	1.2	1010	0.03	0.04	0.8	0
152	Tourtière (Pork pie) (1/6 of 9″ pie)	1 piece	139	—	451	15	34	10	19	4	21	18	2.7	10	0.16	0.09	4.0	—

4. If bones are discarded, value will be greatly reduced.

No.	Food	Measure	Weight	Moisture	Food Energy	Protein	Fat	Fatty Acids: Saturated (Total)	Fatty Acids: Unsaturated: Oleic	Fatty Acids: Unsaturated: Lin-Oleic	Carbohydrate	Calcium	Iron	Vitamin A Value	Thiamine	Riboflavin	Niacin	Ascorbic Acid
			g.	%	Cal	g.	g.	g.	g.	g.	g.	mg.	mg.	I.U.	mg.	mg.	mg.	mg.
	MATURE DRY BEANS AND PEAS, NUTS: RELATED PRODUCTS																	
153	Almonds, shelled, whole	1 cup	142	5	850	26	77	6	52	15	28	332	6.7	0	0.34	1.31	5.0	0
	Beans, dry:																	
154	Cooked, drained, common white	1 cup	180	69	210	14	1	—	—	—	38	90	4.9	0	0.25	0.13	1.3	0
	Canned, solids and liquid																	
	White with																	
155	Wieners (sliced)	1 cup	255	71	365	19	18	—	—	—	32	94	4.8	330	0.18	0.15	3.3	tr.
156	Pork and Tomato Sauce	1 cup	255	71	310	16	7	2	3	1	49	138	4.6	330	0.20	0.08	1.5	5
157	Red Kidney, canned	1 cup	255	76	230	15	1	—	—	—	42	74	4.6	10	0.13	0.10	1.5	—
158	Cashew Nuts, roasted	1 cup	140	5	785	24	64	11	45	4	41	53	5.3	140	0.60	0.35	2.5	—
159	Coconut, shredded, dried, packed	1 cup	62	4	344	2	24	21	2	tr.	33	27	2.2	0	0.02	0.09	0.4	0
160	Lentils, cooked	1 cup	150	69	159	12	tr.	—	—	—	29	38	3.2	30	0.11	0.09	0.9	0
161	Lima Beans, cooked, drained	1 cup	190	64	260	16	1	—	—	—	49	55	5.9	—	0.25	0.11	1.3	—
162	Peanuts, roasted, salted, halves (10¢ bag = ¼ — ⅓c = 40 gr.)	1 cup	144	2	840	37	72	16	31	21	27	107	3.0	—	0.46	0.19	24.7	0
163	Peanut butter	1 Tbsp.	16	2	95	4	8	2	4	2	3	9	0.3	—	0.02	0.02	2.4	0
164	Peas, split, dry cooked	1 cup	250	70	290	20	1	—	—	—	52	28	4.2	100	0.37	0.22	2.2	0
165	Pecans, halves	1 cup	108	3	740	10	77	5	48	15	16	79	2.6	140	0.93	0.14	1.0	0
166	Walnuts, English, halves	1 cup	100	4	650	15	64	4	10	40	16	99	3.1	30	0.33	0.13	0.9	—
167	Walnuts, English, chopped	1 Tbsp.	8	4	50	1	5	tr.	1	3	1	8	0.2	tr.	0.03	0.01	0.1	—
	VEGETABLE AND VEGETABLE PRODUCTS																	
	Asparagus, green:																	
	Cooked, drained																	
168	Spears, ½″ diam. at base	4 spears	60	94	10	1	tr.	—	—	—	2	13	0.4	540	0.10	0.11	0.8	16
169	Pieces, 1½-2″ lengths	1 cup	145	94	30	3	tr.	—	—	—	5	30	0.9	1310	0.23	0.26	2.0	38
170	Canned, drained	1 cup	145	94	30	3	tr.	—	—	—	5	30	2.4	1240	0.09	0.15	1.2	22

	Beans:																	
171	Lima, immature seeds, cooked, drained	1 cup	170	71	190	13	1	—	—	—	34	80	4.3	480	0.31	0.17	2.2	29
	Snap:																	
	Green:																	
172	Cooked, drained	1 cup	125	92	30	2	tr.	—	—	—	7	63	0.8	680	0.09	0.11	0.6	15
173	Canned, drained	1 cup	125	92	30	2	tr.	—	—	—	7	56	1.9	590	0.04	0.06	0.4	5
	Yellow or Wax:																	
174	Cooked, drained	1 cup	125	93	30	2	tr.	—	—	—	6	63	0.8	290	0.09	0.11	0.6	16
175	Canned, drained	1 cup	125	92	30	2	tr.	—	—	—	7	56	1.9	125	0.04	0.06	0.4	6
176	Sprouted, mung beans, cooked	1 cup	125	91	35	4	tr.	—	—	—	7	21	1.1	30	0.11	0.13	0.9	8
	Beets:																	
177	Cooked, diced or sliced	1 cup	170	91	55	2	tr.	—	—	—	12	24	0.9	30	0.05	0.07	0.5	10
178	Canned, drained	1 cup	166	91	62	2	tr.	—	—	—	14	32	1.2	40	0.02	0.04	0.2	6
179	Beet Greens, cooked, drained	1 cup	145	94	25	3	tr.	—	—	—	5	144	2.8	7400	0.10	0.22	0.4	22
	Broccoli, cooked, drained:																	
180	Whole stalks, med. size	1 stalk	180	91	45	6	1	—	—	—	8	158	1.4	4500	0.16	0.36	1.4	162
181	Stalks, cut in ½″ pieces	1 cup	155	91	40	5	1	—	—	—	7	136	1.2	3880	0.14	0.31	1.2	140
182	Brussels Sprouts, cooked, 7-8 sprouts per cup	1 cup	155	88	55	7	1	—	—	—	10	50	1.7	810	0.12	0.22	1.2	135
	Cabbage, common varieties:																	
183	Raw, finely shredded	1 cup	90	92	20	1	tr.	—	—	—	5	44	0.4	120	0.05	0.05	0.3	42
184	Cooked, finely shredded, small amount water	1 cup	170	94	35	2	tr.	—	—	—	6	64	0.4	190	0.06	0.06	0.4	48
185	Cabbage, red, raw, shredded	1 cup	70	90	20	1	tr.	—	—	—	5	29	0.6	30	0.06	0.04	0.3	43
	Carrots:																	
	Raw:																	
186	Whole, 5½ by 1″	1 carrot	50	88	20	1	tr.	—	—	—	5	18	0.4	5500	0.03	0.03	0.3	4
187	Grated	1 cup	110	88	45	1	tr.	—	—	—	11	41	0.8	12100	0.06	0.06	0.7	9
188	Cooked, diced	1 cup	145	91	45	1	tr.	—	—	—	10	48	0.9	15220	0.08	0.07	0.7	9
189	Canned, strained or chopped (baby food)	1 oz.	28	92	10	tr.	tr.	—	—	—	2	7	0.1	3690	0.01	0.01	0.1	1
	Celery, raw:																	
191	Stalk, large, outer, 8 by 1½″	1 stalk	40	94	5	tr.	tr.	—	—	—	2	16	0.1	100	0.01	0.01	0.1	4
192	Pieces, diced	1 cup	100	94	17	1	tr.	—	—	—	4	39	0.3	240	0.03	0.03	0.3	9
193	Celery, cooked, pieces	⅘ cup	100	94	14	1	tr.	—	—	—	3	31	0.2	230	0.03	0.03	0.3	6
	Corn, sweet:																	
194	Cooked, ear 5 by 1¾″	1 ear	140	74	70	3	1	—	—	—	16	2	0.5	310	0.09	0.08	1.0	7
195	Canned, kernels, drained	1 cup	166	79	140	4	tr.	—	—	—	32	8	0.8	580	0.04	0.08	1.4	8
196	Canned, cream style	1 cup	230	82	172	4	tr.	—	—	—	36	10	1.2	460	0.06	0.12	2.0	12

	Food	Measure	Weight	Moisture	Food Energy	Protein	Fat	Fatty Acids: Saturated (Total)	Fatty Acids: Unsaturated: Oleic	Fatty Acids: Unsaturated: Lin-Oleic	Carbohydrate	Calcium	Iron	Vitamin A Value	Thiamine	Riboflavin	Niacin	Ascorbic Acid
			g.	%	Cal	g.	g.	g.	g.	g.	g.	mg.	mg.	I.U.	mg.	mg.	mg.	mg.
	VEGETABLE AND VEGETABLE PRODUCTS (Continued)																	
	Cucumbers, 10 ounce; 7½ by 2″																	
197	Raw, pared, center slice, ⅛″ thick	6 slices	50	96	5	tr.	tr.	—	—	—	2	8	0.2	tr.	0.02	0.02	0.1	6
198	Eggplant, cooked, slices ½″ thick, 4 slices	1 cup	200	19	38	2	0	0	0	0	0	22	1.2	20	0.10	0.08	1.0	6
	Lettuce, raw:																	
199	Crisphead, as Iceberg, head 4¾″ diam.	1 head	454	96	60	4	tr.	—	—	—	13	91	2.3	1500	0.29	0.27	1.3	29
200	Looseleaf, leaves	2 large	50	94	10	1	tr.	—	—	—	2	34	0.7	950	0.03	0.04	0.2	9
201	Mushrooms, canned, solids and liquid	1 cup	244	93	40	5	tr.	—	—	—	6	15	1.2	tr.	0.04	0.60	4.8	4
202	Fresh, sautéed	4 avg.	70	93	78	2	7	3	2	tr.	3	8	0.7	170	0.05	0.28	2.9	tr.
	Onions:																	
	Mature:																	
203	Raw, onion 2½″ diam.	1 onion	110	89	40	2	tr.	—	—	—	10	30	0.6	40	0.04	0.04	0.2	11
204	Cooked	1 cup	210	92	60	3	tr.	—	—	—	14	50	0.8	80	0.06	0.06	0.4	14
205	Fried	½ cup	214	92	176	3	11	6	4	tr.	17	57	1.0	540	0.06	0.08	0.4	20
206	Young green, small without tops	6 onions	50	88	20	1	tr.	—	—	—	5	20	0.3	tr.	0.02	0.02	0.2	12
207	Parsley, raw, chopped	1 Tbsp.	4	85	tr.	tr.	tr.	—	—	—	tr.	8	0.2	340	tr.	0.01	tr.	7
208	Parsnips, cooked	1 cup	155	82	100	2	1	—	—	—	23	70	0.9	50	0.11	0.12	0.2	16
	Peas, green:																	
209	Cooked	1 cup	160	82	115	9	1	—	—	—	19	37	2.9	860	0.44	0.17	3.7	33
210	Canned, drained	1 cup	140	79	112	9	1	—	—	—	20	33	2.9	890	0.16	0.09	1.5	12
211	Canned, strained (baby food)	1 oz.	28	86	15	1	tr.	—	—	—	3	3	0.4	140	0.02	0.02	0.4	3
212	Peppers, hot, red, dried, powder	1 Tbsp.	15	8	50	2	2	—	—	—	8	40	2.3	9750	0.03	0.17	1.3	2
	Peppers, sweet:																	
	Raw, about 5 per pound																	
213	Green, without seeds	1 pod	74	93	15	1	tr.	—	—	—	4	7	0.5	310	0.06	0.06	0.4	94
214	Cooked, boiled, drained	1 pod	73	95	15	1	tr.	—	—	—	3	7	0.4	310	0.05	0.05	0.4	70
	Potatoes, medium (about 3 per pound, raw):																	
215	Baked, peeled after baking	1 potato	99	75	90	3	tr.	—	—	—	21	9	0.7	tr.	0.10	0.04	1.7	20
	Boiled,																	

216	Peeled after boiling	1 potato	136	80	105	3	tr.	—	—	—	23	10	0.8	tr.	0.13	0.05	2.0	22[6]
217	Peeled before boiling	1 potato	122	83	80	2	tr.	—	—	—	18	7	0.6	tr.	0.11	0.04	1.4	20[6]
	French Fried, piece 2″ × ½″ × ½″																	
218	Cooked in deep fat	10 pieces	57	45	155	2	7	2	2	4	20	9	0.7	tr.	0.07	0.04	1.8	12[6]
219	Frozen, heated	10 pieces	57	53	125	2	5	1	1	2	19	5	1.0	tr.	0.08	0.01	1.5	12[6]
	Mashed:																	
220	Milk added	1 cup	195	83	125	4	1	—	—	—	25	47	0.8	50	0.16	0.10	2.0	19[6]
221	Milk and butter added	1 cup	195	80	185	4	8	4	3	tr.	24	47	0.8	330	0.16	0.10	1.9	18[6]
222	Potato chips medium, 2″ diameter, (1 bag, 10¢ = 40 gr.)	10 chips	20	2	115	1	8	2	2	4	10	8	0.4	tr.	0.04	0.01	1.0	3
223	Pumpkin, canned	1 cup	228	90	75	2	1	—	—	—	18	57	0.9	14590	0.07	0.12	1.3	12
224	Radishes, raw, small, without tops	4	40	94	5	tr.	tr.	—	—	—	1	12	0.4	tr.	0.01	0.01	0.1	10
225	Sauerkraut, canned, solids and liquid	1 cup	235	93	45	2	tr.	—	—	—	9	85	1.2	120	0.07	0.09	0.4	33
	Spinach:																	
226	Cooked	1 cup	180	92	40	5	1	—	—	—	6	167	4.0	14580	0.13	0.25	1.0	50
227	Canned, drained solids	1 cup	180	91	45	5	1	—	—	—	6	212	4.7	14400	0.03	0.21	0.6	24
	Squash:																	
	Cooked:																	
228	Summer, diced	1 cup	210	96	30	2	tr.	—	—	—	7	52	0.8	820	0.10	0.16	1.6	21
229	Winter, mashed.	1 cup	205	81	130	4	1	—	—	—	32	57	1.6	8610	0.10	0.27	1.4	27
	Sweet potatoes:																	
	Cooked, medium, 5 by 2 inches, weight raw about 6 ounces:																	
230	Baked, peeled after baking	1 potato	110	64	155	2	1	—	—	—	36	44	1.0	8910	0.10	0.07	0.7	24
231	Boiled, peeled after boiling	1 potato	147	71	170	2	1	—	—	—	39	47	1.0	11610	0.13	0.09	0.9	25
232	Candied, 3½″ × 2¼″	1 potato	175	60	295	2	6	2	3	1	60	65	1.6	11030	0.10	0.08	0.8	17
233	Canned, vacuum or solid pack	1 cup	218	72	235	4	tr.	—	—	—	54	54	1.7	17000	0.10	0.10	1.4	30
	Tomatoes:																	
234	Raw: 2″ × 2½″, 3/lb. or 7-8 miniatures	1 tomato	150	94	35	2	tr.	—	—	—	7	20	0.8	1350	0.10	0.06	1.0	34
235	Canned, solids and liquid	1 cup	241	94	50	2	1	—	—	—	10	14	1.2	2170	0.12	0.07	1.7	41
236	Tomato aspic	½ cup	120	94	32	3	tr.	—	—	—	5	9	1.1	970	0.07	0.04	0.9	20
237	Tomato catsup	1 Tbsp.	15	69	15	tr.	tr.	—	—	—	4	4	0.1	240	0.02	0.01	0.3	3
238	Tomato juice, canned	1 cup	243	94	45	2	tr.	—	—	—	10	17	2.2	1940	0.13	0.07	1.8	39
239	Tomato sauce, canned	¼ cup	68	82	79	1	6	—	—	—	6	7	0.4	870	0.03	0.03	0.5	5

6. Ascorbic acid values can range from about 26 mg per 100 grams in recently dug potatoes to about 12 after 3 months storage and about 8 after 6 months storage.

	Food	Measure	Weight	Moisture	Food Energy	Protein	Fat	Fatty Acids: Saturated (Total)	Fatty Acids: Unsaturated Oleic	Fatty Acids: Unsaturated Lin-Oleic	Carbohydrate	Calcium	Iron	Vitamin A Value	Thiamine	Riboflavin	Niacin	Ascorbic Acid
			g.	%	Cal	g.	g.	g.	g.	g.	g.	mg.	mg.	I.U.	mg.	mg.	mg.	mg.
	VEGETABLE AND VEGETABLE PRODUCTS (Continued)																	
	Turnips (Yellow Rutabagas)																	
240	Raw, sliced (3½″ diam., ⅓″ thick)	¾ cup	100	87	46	1	tr.	—	—	—	11	66	0.5	580	0.07	0.07	1.1	43
241	Cooked, cubes	½ cup	100	91	35	1	tr.	—	—	—	8	59	0.03	550	0.06	0.06	0.5	26
242	Vegetable juice, canned	1 cup	243	94	43	2	tr.	—	—	—	9	30	1.2	1750	0.13	0.08	2.0	23
	PICKLES																	
243	Assorted, sweet	2 pieces	20	—	6	tr.	tr.	—	—	—	1	6	0.5	—	—	—	—	—
244	Dill pickles (4″ × 1¾″)	1 pickle	135	93	15	1	tr.	—	—	—	3	35	1.4	140	tr.	0.03	tr.	8
245	Gherkins (2¾″ × ¾″)	1 pickle	20	61	30	tr.	tr.	—	—	—	7	2	0.2	20	tr.	tr.	tr.	1
246	Olives—Black—large	2 large	10	73	15	tr.	2	tr.	2	tr.	tr.	9	0.1	10	tr.	tr.	—	—
247	Green—medium	4 medium	16	78	15	tr.	2	tr.	2	tr.	tr.	8	0.2	40	—	—	—	—
248	Relish	1 Tbsp.	13	—	14	tr.	tr.	—	—	—	3	2	0.2	10	tr.	tr.	tr.	1
	FRUIT AND FRUIT PRODUCTS																	
249	Apples, raw (3 per pound) 2½″ diam.[5]	1 apple	150	85	70	tr.	tr.	—	—	—	18	8	0.4	50	0.04	0.02	0.1	3
250	Apple juice, canned, vitaminized	1 cup	248	88	120	tr.	tr.	—	—	—	30	15	1.5	—	0.02	0.04	0.2	88*
	Applesauce, canned:																	
251	Sweetened	1 cup	255	76	230	1	tr.	—	—	—	61	10	1.3	100	0.05	0.03	0.1	3
252	Unsweetened	1 cup	244	88	100	1	tr.	—	—	—	26	10	1.2	100	0.05	0.02	0.1	2
	Apricots:																	
253	Raw (about 12 per pound)[5]	3 apricots	114	85	55	1	tr.	—	—	—	14	18	0.5	2890	0.03	0.04	0.7	10
254	Canned in heavy syrup	1 cup	259	77	220	2	tr.	—	—	—	57	28	0.8	4510	0.05	0.06	0.9	10
255	Dried, uncooked (40 halves per cup)	1 cup	150	25	390	8	1	—	—	—	100	100	8.2	16350	0.02	0.23	4.9	19
256	Cooked, unsweetened, fruit & liquid	1 cup	285	76	240	5	1	—	—	—	62	63	5.1	8550	0.01	0.13	2.8	8
257	Apricot nectar, canned	1 cup	251	85	140	1	tr.	—	—	—	37	23	0.5	2380	0.03	0.03	0.5	6
	Avocados, whole fruit, raw;[5]																	
258	California (3⅛″ diam.)	1 avocado	284	74	370	5	37	7	17	5	13	22	1.3	630	0.24	0.43	3.5	30
259	Florida (3⅝″ diam.)	1 avocado	454	78	390	4	33	7	15	4	27	30	1.8	880	0.33	0.61	4.9	43

260	Bananas, raw, medium size[5], 7" - 8" long	1 banana	175	76	100	1	tr.	—	—	—	26	10	0.8	230	0.06	0.07	0.8	12
261	Blackberries, raw	1 cup	144	84	85	2	1	—	—	—	19	46	1.3	290	0.05	0.06	0.5	30
262	Blueberries, raw	1 cup	140	83	85	1	1	—	—	—	21	21	1.4	140	0.04	0.08	0.6	20
263	Cantaloup, raw, medium 5" diameter[5]	½ melon	385	91	60	1	tr.	—	—	—	14	27	0.8	6540	0.08	0.06	1.2	63
	Cherries, canned, red, sour																	
264	Pitted, water pack	1 cup	244	88	105	2	tr.	—	—	—	26	37	0.7	1660	0.07	0.05	0.5	12
265	Cranberry juice cocktail	1 cup	250	83	165	tr.	tr.	—	—	—	42	13	0.8	tr.	0.03	0.03	0.1	40*
266	Cranberry sauce, sweetened, canned, strained	1 cup	277	62	330	tr.	1	—	—	—	85	14	0.5	50	0.02	0.02	0.1	5
267	Dates, pitted, cut	1 cup	178	22	490	4	1	—	—	—	130	105	5.3	90	0.16	0.17	3.9	0
268	Figs, dried, large, 2" by 1"	1 fig	21	23	60	1	tr.	—	—	—	15	26	0.6	20	0.02	0.02	0.1	0
269	Fruit cocktail, canned, heavy syrup	1 cup	256	80	195	1	tr.	—	—	—	50	23	1.0	360	0.05	0.03	1.3	5
	Grapefruit:																	
	Raw, medium 3¾" diam.[5]																	
270	White	½ grapefruit	241	89	45	1	tr.	—	—	—	12	19	0.5	10	0.05	0.02	0.2	44
271	Pink	½ grapefruit	241	89	50	1	tr.	—	—	—	13	20	0.5	540	0.05	0.02	0.2	44
272	Canned, syrup pack	1 cup	250	81	180	2	tr.	—	—	—	45	33	0.8	30	0.08	0.05	0.5	76
	Grapefruit juice:																	
273	Fresh, white	1 cup	246	90	95	1	tr.	—	—	—	23	22	0.5	20	0.09	0.04	0.4	92
	Canned, white:																	
274	Unsweetened	1 cup	247	89	100	1	tr.	—	—	—	24	20	1.0	20	0.07	0.04	0.4	84
275	Sweetened	1 cup	250	86	130	1	tr.	—	—	—	32	20	1.0	20	0.07	0.04	0.4	78
	Frozen, concentrate, unsweetened:																	
276	Undiluted, can, 6 fluid ounces	1 can	207	62	300	4	1	—	—	—	72	70	0.8	60	0.29	0.12	1.4	286
277	Diluted with 3 parts water	1 cup	247	89	100	1	tr.	—	—	—	24	25	0.2	20	0.10	0.04	0.5	96
	Grapes, raw:																	
278	Canadian type (slip skin)	1 cup	153	82	65	1	1	—	—	—	15	15	0.4	100	0.05	0.03	0.2	3
279	European type (adherent skin)	1 cup	160	81	95	1	tr.	—	—	—	25	17	0.6	140	0.07	0.04	0.4	6
	Grape juice:																	
280	Canned or bottled	1 cup	253	83	165	1	tr.	—	—	—	42	28	0.8	—	0.10	0.05	0.5	40*
	Frozen concentrate, sweetened																	
281	Undiluted can, 6 fluid ounces	1 can	216	53	395	1	tr.	0	0	0	97	21	0.8	40	0.13	0.21	1.5	126*
282	Diluted with 3 parts water	1 cup	250	86	135	tr.	tr.	0	0	0	33	8	0.2	10	0.05	0.08	0.5	42*
283	Lemons, raw, 2⅛" diam.[5]	1 lemon	110	90	20	1	tr.	—	—	—	6	19	0.4	10	0.03	0.01	0.1	39
284	Lemon juice, raw	1 cup	244	91	60	1	tr.	—	—	—	20	17	0.5	40	0.07	0.02	0.2	112
285	Lemon juice, canned, unsweetened	1 cup	245	92	55	1	tr.	—	—	—	19	17	0.5	40	0.07	0.03	0.2	102

* Added by Manufacturer in accordance with Food and Drug Regulations.

5. Measure and weight apply to entire fruit or vegetable including parts not usually eaten.

	Food	Measure	Weight	Moisture	Food Energy	Protein	Fat	Fatty Acids: Saturated (Total)	Fatty Acids: Unsaturated: Oleic	Fatty Acids: Unsaturated: Lin-Oleic	Carbohydrate	Calcium	Iron	Vitamin A Value	Thiamine	Riboflavin	Niacin	Ascorbic Acid
	FRUIT AND FRUIT PRODUCTS (Continued)		g.	%	Cal	g.	g.	g.	g.	g.	g.	mg.	mg.	I.U.	mg.	mg.	mg.	mg.
	Lemonade concentrate:																	
286	Frozen, 6 fl. oz. per can	1 can	219	48	430	tr.	tr.	—	—	—	112	9	0.4	40	0.04	0.07	0.7	66
287	Diluted with 4⅓ parts water	1 cup	248	88	110	tr.	tr.	—	—	—	28	2	tr.	10	tr.	0.02	0.2	17
	Lime juice:																	
288	Fresh	1 cup	246	90	65	1	tr.	—	—	—	22	22	0.5	20	0.05	0.02	0.2	79
289	Canned, unsweetened	1 cup	246	90	65	1	tr.	—	—	—	22	22	0.5	20	0.05	0.02	0.2	52
290	Oranges, raw, 2⅝″ diam.[5]	1 orange	180	86	65	1	tr.	—	—	—	16	54	0.5	260	0.13	0.05	0.5	66
291	Orange juice, fresh, all varieties	1 cup	248	88	110	2	1	—	—	—	26	27	0.5	500	0.22	0.07	1.0	124
292	Canned, unsweetened	1 cup	249	87	120	2	tr.	—	—	—	28	25	1.0	500	0.17	0.05	0.7	100
	Frozen concentrate:																	
293	Undiluted, can, 6 fl. oz.	1 can	213	55	360	5	tr.	—	—	—	87	75	0.9	1620	0.68	0.11	2.8	360
294	Diluted with 3 parts water	1 cup	249	87	120	2	tr.	—	—	—	29	25	0.2	550	0.22	0.02	1.0	120
	Orange and grapefruit juice:																	
295	Canned, sweetened	1 cup	251	—	130	1	tr.	—	—	—	35	23	0.8	100	0.13	0.05	0.5	95
	Frozen concentrate:																	
296	Undiluted, can, 6 fl. oz.	1 can	210	59	330	4	1	—	—	—	78	61	0.8	790	0.47	0.06	2.3	301
297	Diluted with 3 parts water	1 cup	248	88	110	1	tr.	—	—	—	26	20	0.2	270	0.16	0.02	0.8	102
	Peaches:																	
	Raw:																	
298	Whole, medium, 2″ diam. 4 per lb.[5]	1 peach	114	89	35	1	tr.	—	—	—	10	9	0.5	1320	0.02	0.05	1.0	7
299	Sliced	1 cup	168	89	65	1	tr.	—	—	—	16	15	0.8	2230	0.03	0.08	1.6	12
	Canned, solids and liquid:																	
	Syrup pack, heavy:																	
300	Halves or slices	1 cup	257	79	200	1	tr.	—	—	—	52	10	0.8	1100	0.02	0.06	1.4	7
301	Water pack	1 cup	245	91	75	1	tr.	—	—	—	20	10	0.7	1100	0.02	0.06	1.4	7
302	Dried, uncooked	1 cup	160	25	420	5	1	—	—	—	109	77	9.6	6240	0.02	0.31	8.5	28
303	Cooked, unsweetened	1 cup	270	77	220	3	1	—	—	—	58	41	5.1	3290	0.01	0.15	4.2	6
304	Frozen, carton, 12 ounces	1 carton	340	76	300	1	tr.	—	—	—	77	14	1.7	2210	0.03	0.14	2.4	135

	Pears:																	
305	Raw, 3″ × 2½″ diam.[5]	1 pear	182	83	100	1	1	—	—	—	25	13	0.5	30	0.04	0.07	0.2	7
	Canned, solids and liquid:																	
	Syrup pack, heavy:																	
306	Halves or slices	1 cup	255	80	195	1	1	—	—	—	50	13	0.5	tr.	0.03	0.05	0.3	4
	Pineapple:																	
307	Raw, diced	1 cup	140	85	75	1	tr.	—	—	—	19	24	0.7	100	0.12	0.04	0.3	24
	Canned, heavy syrup, solids and liquid:																	
308	Crushed	1 cup	260	80	195	1	tr.	—	—	—	50	29	0.8	120	0.20	0.06	0.5	17
309	Sliced—large, with juice	1 slice	122	80	90	tr.	tr.	—	—	—	24	13	0.4	50	0.09	0.03	0.2	8
310	Pineapple juice, canned	1 cup	249	86	135	1	tr.	—	—	—	34	37	0.7	120	0.12	0.04	0.5	22[1]
	Plums:[5]																	
311	Raw, 2″ diam., about 2 ounces	1 plum	60	87	25	tr.	tr.	—	—	—	7	7	0.3	140	0.02	0.02	0.3	3
312	Canned, syrup pack (with pits) and juice	1 cup	256	77	205	1	tr.	—	—	—	53	22	2.2	2970	0.05	0.05	0.9	4
	Prunes, dried, "softenized", medium:																	
313	Uncooked[5]	4 prunes	32	28	70	1	tr.	—	—	—	18	14	1.1	440	0.02	0.04	0.4	1
314	Cooked, unsweetened	1 cup	270	66	295	2	1	—	—	—	78	60	4.5	1860	0.08	0.18	1.7	2
315	Prune juice, canned or bottled	1 cup	256	80	200	1	tr.	—	—	—	49	36	10.5	—	0.03	0.03	1.0	5
	Raisins, seedless:																	
316	Packaged, ½ oz. or 1½ tbsp. per pkg.	1 pkg.	14	18	40	tr.	tr.	—	—	—	11	9	0.5	tr.	0.02	0.01	0.1	tr.
317	Cup, pressed down	1 cup	165	18	480	4	tr.	—	—	—	128	102	5.8	30	0.18	0.13	0.8	2
	Raspberries:																	
318	Raw	1 cup	123	84	70	1	1	—	—	—	17	27	1.1	160	0.04	0.11	1.1	31
319	Frozen—10 oz. carton	1 carton	284	74	275	2	1	—	—	—	70	37	1.7	200	0.06	0.17	1.7	59
320	Rhubarb, cooked, sugar added	1 cup	272	63	385	1	tr.	—	—	—	98	212	1.6	220	0.06	0.15	0.7	17
	Strawberries:																	
321	Raw, capped	1 cup	149	90	55	1	1	—	—	—	13	31	1.5	90	0.04	0.10	1.0	88
322	Frozen, 10 oz. carton	1 carton	284	71	310	1	1	—	—	—	79	40	2.0	90	0.06	0.17	1.5	150
323	Tangerines, raw, medium, 2⅜″ diam.[5]	1 tangerine	116	87	40	1	tr.	—	—	—	10	34	0.3	360	0.05	0.02	0.1	27
	Tangerine juice, frozen, concentrated:																	
324	6 oz. can	1 can	210	58	340	4	1	—	—	—	80	130	1.5	3070	0.43	0.12	0.9	202
325	Diluted with 3 parts water	1 cup	248	88	115	1	tr.	—	—	—	27	45	0.5	1020	0.14	0.04	0.3	67
326	Canned, unsweetened	1 cup	248	89	105	1	tr.	—	—	—	25	45	0.5	1040	0.14	0.04	0.3	56
	Watermelon, raw, wedge 4″ × 8″[5]																	
327	(1/16 of 10″ × 16″ watermelon) or slice (8¾″ diam. × 1″ thick)	1 wedge	925	93	115	2	1	—	—	—	27	30	2.1	2510	0.13	0.13	0.7	30

1. Value applies to unfortified product. Refer to label for information concerning addition of vitamins.
5. Measure and weight apply to entire fruit or vegetable including parts not usually eaten.

	Food	Measure	Weight	Moisture	Food Energy	Protein	Fat	Fatty Acids: Saturated (Total)	Fatty Acids: Unsaturated: Oleic	Fatty Acids: Unsaturated: Lin-Oleic	Carbohydrate	Calcium	Iron	Vitamin A Value	Thiamine	Riboflavin	Niacin	Ascorbic Acid
			g.	%	Cal	g.	g.	g.	g.	g.	g.	mg.	mg.	I.U.	mg.	mg.	mg.	mg.
	FRUIT AND FRUIT PRODUCTS (Continued)																	
	Fruit and Fruit Flavoured Breakfast Drinks																	
	Canned or bottled with added Vitamin C																	
328	Individual fruit flavors or combinations of two or more	1 cup	250	90	135	tr.	tr.	—	—	—	35	12	0.5	130	0.05	0.02	0.2	40*
	Made with crystals with added Vitamin C																	
329	Orange, grapefruit, apple etc. (Start, Tang, etc.)	1 cup	248	—	135	tr.	tr.	—	—	—	35	—	—	—	—	—	—	40*
	CEREALS AND CEREAL PRODUCTS																	
330	Barley, pearled, light, uncooked	1 cup	200	11	700	16	2	tr.	1	1	158	32	4.0	0	0.24	0.10	6.2	0
331	Biscuits, baking powder, 2″ diam., enriched flour	1 biscuit	28	27	105	2	5	1	2	1	13	34	0.4	tr.	0.06	0.06	0.1	—
332	Bran flakes, with added nutrients	¾ cup	28	3	104	3	tr.	—	—	—	22	13	4.0*	0	0.60*	1.00*	6.0*	0
333	Branflakes, with raisins & nutrients	⅔ cup	28	3	100	2	tr.	—	—	—	22	15	4.0*	0	0.60*	1.00*	6.0*	0
	Breads:																	
334	Cracked Wheat	1 slice	30	35	77	3	1	tr.	tr.	tr.	15	25	0.3	0	0.03	0.03	0.4	0
335	Melba toast	1 piece	4	4	15	tr.	tr.	—	—	—	3	—	—	—	—	—	—	—
336	Raisin—18 slices per loaf	1 slice	25	35	65	2	tr.	—	—	—	13	18	0.3	0	0.01	0.02	0.2	—
337	Rye, light	1 slice	30	35	73	3	—	—	—	—	16	22	0.5	0	0.05	0.02	0.4	0
338	Rye, dark, pumpernickel	1 slice	32	34	79	3	tr.	—	—	—	17	27	0.8	0	0.07	0.04	0.4	0
339	White, enriched, 24 slices per loaf	1 slice	30	35	82	2	1	—	—	—	15	20	0.5	0	0.07	0.05	0.7	0
340	White, enriched (Newfoundland)[3]	1 slice	30	35	82	2	1	—	—	—	15	35	0.5	0	0.07	0.5	0.7	0
341	Whole wheat (60% whole wheat)	1 slice	30	35	72	3	1	—	—	—	15	15	0.7	0	0.05	0.03	1.0	0
342	Breadcrumbs, dry, grated	1 cup	100	6	390	6	1	—	—	—	78	11	1.0	0	0.08	0.05	4.1	0
	Cakes made from cake mixes:																	
	Angelfood:																	
343	Piece, 1/12 of 10-in. diam. cake	1 piece	53	34	135	3	—	—	—	—	32	50	0.2	0	tr.	0.06	0.1	0

	Devil's food, 2-layer, with chocolate icing																
344	Piece, 1/16 of 9-in. diam. cake	1 piece	69	24	235	3	9	3	4	1	40	41	0.6	100	0.02	0.06	0.2	0
345	Cupcake, small, 2½ in. diam.	1 cupcake	35	24	120	2	4	1	2	tr.	20	21	0.3	50	0.01	0.03	0.1	0
	Gingerbread																
346	Piece, 1/9 of 8-in. square cake	1 piece	63	37	175	2	4	1	2	1	32	57	1.0	tr.	0.02	0.06	0.5	0
	White, 2-layer, with chocolate icing:																
347	Piece, 1/16 of 9-in. diam. cake	1 piece	71	21	250	3	8	3	3	1	45	70	0.4	40	0.01	0.06	0.1	0
	Cakes made from home recipes:																
348	Boston cream pie; piece 1/12 of 8-in. diam.	1 piece	69	35	210	4	6	2	3	1	34	46	0.3	140	0.02	0.08	0.1	0
	Fruitcake, dark, made with enriched flour:																
349	Slice, 1/30 of 8-in. loaf	1 slice	15	18	55	1	2	tr.	1	tr.	9	11	0.4	20	0.02	0.02	0.1	0
	Plain sheet cake:																
	Without icing:																
350	Piece, 1/9 of 9-in. square cake	1 piece	86	25	315	4	12	3	6	2	48	55	0.3	150	0.02	0.08	0.2	0
351	With boiled white icing, piece 1/9 of 9-in. square cake	1 piece	114	23	400	4	12	3	6	2	71	56	0.3	150	0.02	0.08	0.2	0
	Pound:																
352	Slice, ½ in. thick	1 slice	30	17	140	2	9	2	4	1	14	6	0.2	80	0.01	0.03	0.1	0
	Sponge:																
353	Piece, 1/12 of 10-in. diam. cake	1 piece	66	32	195	5	4	1	2	tr.	36	20	0.8	300	0.03	0.09	0.1	0
	Yellow, 2-layer, without icing:																
354	Piece, 1/16 of 9-in. diam. cake	1 piece	54	24	200	2	7	2	3	1	32	39	0.2	80	0.01	0.04	0.1	0
	Yellow, 2-layer, with chocolate icing:																
355	Piece, 1/16 of 9-in. diam cake	1 piece	75	21	275	3	10	3	4	1	45	51	0.5	120	0.02	0.06	0.2	0
	Cookies:																
	Brownies with nuts:																
356	Made from home recipe with enriched flour	1 brownie	20	10	95	1	6	1	3	1	10	8	0.4	40	0.04	0.02	0.1	0
	Chocolate chip:																
357	Made from home recipe with enriched flour	1 cookie	10	3	50	1	3	1	1	1	6	4	0.2	10	0.01	0.01	0.1	0
358	Commercial	1 cookie	10	3	50	1	2	1	1	tr.	7	4	0.2	10	tr.	tr.	tr.	0
359	Chocolate Marshmallow	1 biscuit	19	—	75	1	2	—	—	—	14	5	0.3	10	tr.	0.01	tr.	0
360	Fig bars, commercial	1 cookie	14	14	50	1	1	—	—	—	11	11	0.2	20	tr.	0.01	0.1	tr.
361	Sandwich, chocolate or vanilla, commercial	1 cookie	10	2	50	1	2	1	1	tr.	7	2	0.1	0	tr.	tr.	0.1	0
362	Social Tea or Arrowroot	1 biscuit	5	2	20	tr.	1	tr.	tr.	tr.	4	—	—	—	—	—	—	0
363	Oatmeal, Dad's	1 biscuit	19	—	86	1	3	—	—	—	13	—	—	—	—	—	—	0

* Added by Manufacturer in accordance with Food and Drug Regulations.

3. Increased calcium according to Provincial Regulations and Food and Drug Regulations.

No.	Food	Measure	Weight	Moisture	Food Energy	Protein	Fat	Fatty Acids: Saturated (Total)	Fatty Acids: Unsaturated: Oleic	Fatty Acids: Unsaturated: Lin-Oleic	Carbohydrate	Calcium	Iron	Vitamin A Value	Thiamine	Riboflavin	Niacin	Ascorbic Acid
			g.	%	Cal	g.	g.	g.	g.	g.	g.	mg.	mg.	I.U.	mg.	mg.	mg.	mg.
	CEREALS AND CEREAL PRODUCTS (Continued)																	
	Cornflakes:																	
364	Plain	1 cup	21	4	80	2	tr.	—	—	—	17	1	0.2	0	tr.	0.02	0.3	0
365	Sugar coated	1 cup	28	2	107	1	tr.	—	—	—	25	1	0.2	0	0.38	0.8	3.7	0
366	Cornflakes, added nutrients	1 cup	21	4	80	2	tr.	—	—	—	18	1	3.0*	0	0.45*	0.75*	4.5*	0
367	Cornflakes, presweetened, added nutrients	1 cup	28	2	107	1	tr.	—	—	—	25	1	4.0*	0	0.60*	0.80*	6.0*	0
368	Cornmeal, degermed, dry form	1 cup	138	12	500	11	2	—	—	—	108	8	1.5	610	0.19	0.07	1.4	0
369	Corn muffins, made from mix	1 muffin	40	33	125	3	4	1	2	1	20	96	0.6	100	0.07	0.08	0.6	0
370	Corn, puffed, presweetened[1]	1 cup	28	2	108	1	tr.	—	—	—	25	3	0.3	0	0.04	—	0.5	0
371	Corn, puffed, presweetened, added nutrients	1 cup	28	2	110	1	tr.	—	—	—	26	3	4.0*	—	0.60*	—	6.0*	0
372	Corn, shredded, added iron	1 cup	28	4	104	2	tr.	—	—	—	24	2	4.0*	0	—	tr.	0.3	0
	Crackers:																	
373	Graham — 2½″ square	4 crackers	28	6	110	2	3	—	—	—	21	11	0.4	0	0.01	0.06	0.4	0
374	Saltines 2″ square	4 crackers	11	4	50	1	1	—	1	—	8	2	0.1	0	tr.	tr.	0.1	0
375	Danish pastry, plain, round 4½″ diam. by 1″	1 pastry	65	22	275	5	15	5	7	3	30	33	0.6	200	0.05	0.10	0.5	0
376	Date Squares	1 square	90	—	226	2	5	1	3	tr.	45	24	1.3	10	0.07	0.05	0.8	0
377	Doughnuts, cake type, 3″ diam.	1	32	24	125	1	6	1	4	tr.	16	13	0.4	30	0.05	0.05	0.4	0
378	Eclairs, chocolate, custard filling	1	110	—	315	8	15	—	—	—	39	90	1.3	730	0.12	0.24	1.0	0
	Farina, quick cooking, cooked:																	
379	Enriched	1 cup	245	89	105	3	tr.	—	—	—	21	180	15.5*	0	0.05	0.02	0.3	0
380	Unenriched	1 cup	245	89	105	3	tr.	—	—	—	21	8	0.3	0	0.04	0.02	0.2	0
381	Macaroni, cooked	1 cup	140	72	155	5	1	—	—	—	32	11	0.6	0	0.02	0.02	0.4	0
382	Macaroni and cheese, baked	1 cup	220	58	430	18	24	11	10	1	44	398	2.0	950	0.22	0.44	2.0	tr.
	Muffins, with enriched white flour:																	
383	Muffin 3″ diam.	1 muffin	40	38	120	3	4	1	2	1	17	42	0.6	40	0.07	0.09	0.6	tr.
384	Muffins, bran	1 muffin	35	—	86	3	3	tr.	2	tr.	14	35	1.3	60	0.07	0.09	1.5	0
385	Noodles (egg noodles), cooked, unenriched	1 cup	160	70	200	7	2	1	1	tr.	37	16	1.0	110	0.05	0.03	0.6	0
386	Oats, puffed, with or without corn	1 cup	25	3	100	3	1	—	—	—	25	23	1.0	0	0.02	—	0.5	0
387	Oats, puffed, presweetened	¾ cup	25	2	107	2	1	—	—	—	25	23	1.0	0	0.03	0.03	0.4	0

388	Oatmeal or rolled oats, cooked	1 cup	240	87	130	5	2	—	—	—	23	22	1.4	0	0.19	0.05	0.2	0
389	Oatmeal, dry, regular or quick cooking	1 cup	80	—	312	11	6	—	—	—	55	42	3.6	0	0.48	0.11	0.8	0
390	Oatmeal, dry, instant (¾ c. cooked)	1 envelope	28	—	107	5	2	—	—	—	19	14	1.0	0	0.16	0.04	0.3	0
	Pancakes, 4″ diam.:																	
391	Plain, made from mix with egg and milk	1	27	50	60	2	2	1	1	tr.	6	58	0.3	70	0.04	0.06	0.2	—
392	Buckwheat, made from mix with egg and milk	1	27	58	55	2	2	1	1	tr.	6	59	0.4	60	0.03	0.04	0.2	—
	Pie (piecrust made with enriched flour):																	
	Sector, 4″, ⅙ of 9″ pie																	
393	Apple (2-crust)	1 sector	160	—	410	3	18	5	11	1	61	1	0.5	50	0.03	0.03	0.6	2
394	Blueberry (2-crust)	1 sector	160	—	387	4	17	—	—	—	56	18	1.0	50	0.03	0.03	0.5	5
395	Cherry (2-crust)	1 sector	160	—	387	4	18	5	11	1	62	22	0.5	710	0.03	0.03	0.8	tr.
396	Custard (1-crust)	1 sector	150	—	327	9	17	6	10	1	35	144	0.9	350	0.08	0.24	0.4	0
397	Lemon meringue	1 sector	140	—	357	5	14	5	8	1	53	20	0.7	240	0.05	0.11	0.3	4
398	Mince (2-crust)	1 sector	160	43	434	4	18	4	11	1	66	45	1.6	tr.	0.11	0.06	0.6	2
399	Peach (2-crust)	1 sector	165	—	421	4	18	5	11	1	63	16	0.8	1200	0.03	0.07	1.2	5
400	Pumpkin (1-crust)	1 sector	150	—	317	6	17	6	8	1	37	76	0.8	3700	0.04	0.15	0.8	tr.
401	Raisin	1 sector	120	—	325	3	13	—	—	—	33	22	1.1	tr.	0.04	0.04	0.4	1
402	Piecrust, baked shell for pie, made with enriched flour	1 shell	135	15	675	8	45	10	29	3	59	19	2.3	0	0.27	0.19	2.4	0
403	Pizza (cheese) ⅛ of 14″ diam. pie	1 sector 5½″	75	45	185	7	6	2	3	tr.	27	107	0.7	290	0.04	0.12	0.7	4
404	Pizza (sausage) ⅛ of 14″ diam. pie	1 sector 5½″	105	45	315	14	17	2	3	tr.	27	111	1.8	290	0.12	0.18	1.6	4
	Popcorn, popped:																	
405	With oil and salt	1 cup	9	3	40	1	2	1	tr.	tr.	5	1	0.2	—	—	0.01	0.1	0
406	Sugar coated	1 cup	35	4	135	2	1	—	—	—	30	2	0.5	—	—	0.02	0.4	0
	Pretzels:																	
407	Dutch, twisted	1 pretzel	16	5	60	2	1	—	—	—	12	4	0.2	0	tr.	tr.	0.1	0
408	Stick, regular, 3⅛″	5 sticks	3	5	10	tr.	tr.	—	—	—	2	1	tr.	0	—	—	—	0
409	Puff Pastry — 10 shells — 4″ diam.	10 shells	284	—	1198	14	93	50	30	3	79	41	3.2	3750	0.50	0.30	4.0	0
410	Rice, brown, cooked (¼ c. raw)	1 cup	160	71	198	4	tr.	—	—	—	43	18	0.9	0	0.19	0.02	2.6	0
	Rice, white:																	
411	Unenriched, cooked, short grain (¼ c. raw)	1 cup	170	73	215	4	tr.	—	—	—	50	14	0.4	0	0.04	0.02	0.9	0
412	Parboiled, cooked (converted) (¼ c. raw)	1 cup	160	73	185	4	tr.	—	—	—	41	33	1.4	0	0.19	0.02	2.1	0
413	Fried, unenriched, chicken	1 cup	185	73	286	3	11	4	tr.	—	41	21	1.5	460	0.19	0.01	1.6	tr.
414	Rice, puffed or oven popped	1 cup	20	4	78	1	tr.	—	—	—	18	3	0.4	0	0.02	0.01	0.2	0
415	Puffed or oven popped with added nutrients	1 cup	28	4	106	2	tr.	—	—	—	24	5	4.0*	0	0.60*	1.00*	6.0*	0
416	Puffed or oven popped, presweetened	1 cup	28	2	120	1	tr.	—	—	—	25	12	0.2	0	0.02	0.01	0.2	0

* **Added by Manufacturer in accordance with Food and Drug Regulations.**

No.	Food	Measure	Weight	Moisture	Food Energy	Protein	Fat	Fatty Acids: Saturated (Total)	Fatty Acids: Unsaturated Oleic	Fatty Acids: Unsaturated Lin-Oleic	Carbohydrate	Calcium	Iron	Vitamin A Value	Thiamine	Riboflavin	Niacin	Ascorbic Acid
			g.	%	Cal	g.	g.	g.	g.	g.	g.	mg.	mg.	I.U.	mg.	mg.	mg.	mg.
	CEREALS AND CEREAL PRODUCTS (Continued)																	
417	Puffed or oven popped, presweetened with added nutrients	1 cup	28	4	120	1	2	—	—	—	24	5	0.7	0	0.6*	1.00*	6.0*	0
418	Shredded, with added nutrients	1 cup	28	4	108	2	tr.	—	—	—	24	7	4.0*	0	0.6*	—	6.0*	0
	Rolls, enriched:																	
419	Cinnamon	1 roll	50	31	158	3	5	—	—	—	26	27	0.9	210	0.08	0.09	0.8	0
420	Hamburger	1 roll	60	31	164	5	2	tr.	1	tr.	30	40	1.0	0	0.14	0.10	1.4	0
421	Hot dog	1 roll	50	31	137	5	2	tr.	1	tr.	25	33	0.8	0	0.12	0.08	1.2	0
422	Spaghetti, cooked	1 cup	140	72	155	5	1	—	—	—	32	11	0.6	0	0.02	0.02	0.4	0
423	Spaghetti, with meat balls and tomato sauce	1 cup	248	70	330	19	12	4	6	1	39	125	3.8	1600	0.26	0.30	4.0	22
424	Spaghetti, with tomato sauce and cheese, canned	1 cup	250	80	190	6	2	1	1	1	38	40	2.8	930	0.35	0.28	4.5	10
425	Spaghetti, Italian, with meat sauce	1 cup	292	—	396	13	21	—	—	—	39	27	2.1	900	0.12	0.12	3.0	24
426	Waffles, made from mix with egg and milk	7″ diam. waffle	75	41	210	7	7	2	4	1	28	85	1.3	250	0.13	0.19	1.0	0
427	Wheat, flakes	1 cup	28	4	105	3	tr.	—	—	—	23	10	0.8	0	0.02	0.06	1.5	0
428	Wheat flakes, with added nutrients	1 cup	28	4	105	3	tr.	—	—	—	23	10	4.0*	0	0.6*	1.0*	6.0*	0
429	Wheat puffed	1 cup	15	3	55	2	tr.	—	—	—	12	7	0.5	0	tr.	0.03	0.7	0
430	Wheat puffed, presweetened	1 cup	21	3	80	1	tr.	—	—	—	18	2	0.7	0	—	0.02	0.7	0
431	Wheat puffed, presweetened with added nutrients	1 cup	21	3	80	1	tr.	—	—	—	18	2	0.7	0	0.4*	0.75*	4.5*	0
	Wheat flours																	
432	Whole wheat	1 cup	120	12	400	17	2	tr.	tr.	tr.	85	35	3.6	0	0.7	0.20	7.2	0
433	All purpose, enriched	1 cup	110	12	386	13	1	tr.	tr.	tr.	78	18	3.2	0	0.5	0.30	4.0	0
434	Cake	1 cup	100	12	350	9	1	tr.	tr.	tr.	74	18	1.0	0	0.1	0.04	1.0	
435	Wheat, shredded	1 biscuit	25	7	80	1	tr.	—	—	—	18	10	0.8	0	0.06	0.02	1.3	0
	1 biscuit=12 spoon size																	
436	Wheat, shredded, with added nutrients	2/3 cup	30	35	138	3	tr.	—	—	—	27	16	1.0	0	0.6*	1.00*	6.0*	0

	FATS AND OILS																	
437	Butter:	1/2 cup	113	16	812	1	92	51	30	3	1	23	0	3750	—	—	—	0
438	Tablespoon	1 Tbsp.	14	16	100	tr.	12	6	4	tr.	tr.	3	0	470	—	—	—	0
439	Pat (90 per lb)	1 pat	5	16	35	tr.	4	2	1	tr.	tr.	1	0	170	—	—	—	0
	Fats, cooking:																	
440	Lard	1 cup	205	0	1850	0	205	78	94	20	0	0	0	0	0	0	0	0
441	Lard	1 Tbsp.	13	0	115	0	13	5	6	1	0	0	0	0	0	0	0	0
442	Vegetable fats (shortening)	1 cup	200	0	1770	0	200	50	100	44	0	0	0	0	0	0	0	0
443	Vegetable fats (shortening)	1 Tbsp.	13	0	110	0	13	3	6	3	0	0	0	0	0	0	0	0
	Margarine:																	
444	Regular	1/2 cup	113	16	815	1	92	17	46	25	1	23	0	3980*	—	—	—	0
445	Regular	1 Tbsp.	14	16	100	tr.	12	2	6	3	tr.	3	0	490*				
446	Soft, 2-8 oz. tubs per pound	1 tub	227	16	1635	1	184	34	68	68	1	45	0	7960*	—	—	—	0
447	Soft, 2-8 oz. tubs per pound	1 Tbsp.	14	16	100	tr.	11	2	4	4	tr.	3	0	490*	—	—	—	0
448	Oils, salad or cooking, corn	1 cup	220	0	1945	0	220	22	62	117	0	0	0	—	0	0	0	0
449	Oils, salad or cooking, corn	1 Tbsp.	14	0	125	0	14	1	4	7	0	0	0	—	0	0	0	0
	Salad dressings:																	
450	Blue cheese	1 Tbsp.	15	32	75	1	8	2	2	4	1	12	tr.	30	tr.	0.02	tr.	tr.
451	Commercial, mayonnaise type	1 Tbsp.	15	41	65	tr.	6	1	1	3	2	2	tr.	40	tr.	tr.	tr.	0
	French:																	
452	Regular	1 Tbsp.	15	16	59	tr.	6	1	1	3	2	2	tr.		tr.	tr.	tr.	0
453	Low calorie	1 Tbsp.	16	95	13	tr.	tr.	—	—	—	2.2	2	0.1	—	—	—	—	0
454	Home cooked, boiled	1 Tbsp.	16	68	25	1	2	1	1	tr.	2	14	0.1	—	—	—	—	0
455	Mayonnaise	1 Tbsp.	14	15	100	tr.	11	2	2	6	tr.	3	0.1	40	tr.	0.01	tr.	0
456	Thousand Island	1 Tbsp.	16	32	50	tr.	8	1	2	4	3	2	0.1	50	tr.	tr.	tr.	tr.
	SUGARS AND SWEETS																	
	Cake icings:																	
457	Chocolate made with milk and fat	1 cup	275	14	1035	9	38	21	14	1	185	165	3.3	580	0.06	0.28	0.6	1
458	Creamy fudge from mix with water only	1 cup	245	15	830	7	16	5	8	3	183	96	2.7	tr.	0.05	0.20	0.7	tr.
459	White, boiled	1 cup	94	18	300	1	0	—	—	—	76	2	tr.	0	tr.	0.03	tr.	0
	Candy:																	
460	Caramels, plain or chocolate 1=10 g	1 oz.	28	8	115	1	3	2	1	tr.	22	42	0.4	tr.	0.01	0.05	0.1	tr.
461	Chocolate, milk, plain	1 oz.	28	1	145	2	9	5	3	tr.	16	65	0.3	80	0.02	0.10	0.1	tr.
462	Chocolate coated peanuts	1 oz.	28	1	160	5	12	3	6	2	11	33	0.4	tr.	0.10	0.05	2.1	tr.
463	Chocolate fudge	1 oz.	28	8	112	1	3	1	1	1	21	22	0.3	tr.	0.01	0.03	0.1	tr.
464	Chocolate, baking, sweet	1 oz.	28	1	150	1	10	6	4	tr.	16	27	0.4	tr.	0.01	0.04	0.1	tr.

* Added by Manufacturer in accordance with Food and Drug Regulations.

	Food	Measure	Weight	Moisture	Food Energy	Protein	Fat	Fatty Acids Saturated (Total)	Fatty Acids Un-saturated Oleic	Fatty Acids Un-saturated Lin-Oleic	Carbohydrate	Calcium	Iron	Vitamin A Value	Thiamine	Riboflavin	Niacin	Ascorbic Acid
			g.	%	Cal	g.	g.	g.	g.	g.	g.	mg.	mg.	I.U.	mg.	mg.	mg.	mg.
	SUGARS AND SWEETS (Continued)																	
465	Gum drops	1 oz.	28	12	100	tr.	tr.	—	—	—	25	2	0.1	0	0	tr.	tr.	0
466	Hard 1=5 g.	1 oz.	28	1	110	0	tr.	—	—	—	28	6	0.5	0	0	0	0	0
467	Marshmallows 1=8 g.	1 oz.	28	17	90	1	tr.	—	—	—	23	5	0.5	0	0	tr.	tr.	0
	Milk chocolate bars:																	
468	All varieties	1¼ oz.	35	—	168	3	8	5	3	tr.	22	31	0.9	—	0.02	0.06	2.0	0
469	"Caravan", "Caramilk" type	1 oz.	28	8	116	1	4	2	2	tr.	20	36	0.4	10	0.02	0.05	tr.	tr.
470	"Oh Henry" type	1 oz.	28	7	129	3	6	2	3	1	16	36	0.3	tr.	0.07	0.04	1.0	tr.
	Chocolate flavoured syrup:																	
471	Thin type	1 fl. oz.	38	32	90	1	1	—	—	—	24	6	0.6	tr.	0.01	0.03	0.2	0
472	Fudge type	1 fl. oz.	38	25	125	2	5	3	2	tr.	20	48	0.5	60	0.02	0.08	0.2	tr.
	Chocolate-flavoured beverage powder (4 heaping teaspoons per ounce):																	
473	With skim milk powder	1 oz.	28	2	100	5	1	tr.	tr.	tr.	20	167	0.5	10	0.04	0.21	0.2	1
474	Without skim milk powder	1 oz.	28	1	100	1	1	tr.	tr.	tr.	25	9	0.6	—	0.01	0.03	0.1	0
475	Honey strained	1 Tbsp.	21	17	65	tr.	0	—	—	—	17	1	0.1	0	tr.	0.01	0.1	tr.
476	Jams and preserves	1 Tbsp.	20	29	55	tr.	tr.	—	—	—	14	4	0.2	tr.	tr.	0.01	tr.	tr.
477	Jellies	1 Tbsp.	18	29	50	tr.	tr.	—	—	—	13	4	0.3	tr.	tr.	0.01	tr.	1
	Molasses, cane:																	
478	Light (first extraction)	1 Tbsp.	20	24	50	—	—	—	—	—	13	33	0.9	—	0.01	0.01	tr.	—
479	Blackstrap	1 Tbsp.	20	24	45	—	—	—	—	—	11	137	3.2	—	0.02	0.04	0.4	—
	Syrups:																	
480	Table blends	1 Tbsp.	21	24	60	0	0	—	—	—	15	9	0.8	0	0	0	0	0
481	Maple	1 Tbsp.	21	—	50	0	0	—	—	—	13	33	0.6	0	0	0	0	0
	Sugars:																	
482	Brown — firm packed	1 cup	220	2	820	0	0	—	—	—	212	187	7.5	0	0.02	0.07	0.4	0
	White:																	
483	Granulated	1 cup	200	tr.	770	0	0	—	—	—	199	0	0.2	0	0	0	0	0
484	Granulated	1 Tbsp.	11	tr.	40	0	0	—	—	—	11	0	tr.	0	0	0	0	0
485	Powdered, stirred before measuring	1 cup	120	tr.	460	0	0	—	—	—	119	0	0.1	0	0	0	0	0

	MISCELLANEOUS ITEMS																	
486	Barbecue Sauce	1 cup	250	81	230	4	17	2	5	9	20	53	2.0	900	0.03	0.03	0.8	13
	Beverages, alcoholic:																	
487	Beer	12 fl. oz.	360	92	150	1	0	—	—	—	14	18	tr.	—	0.01	0.11	2.2	—
488	Gin, rum, vodka, whiskey	1½ fl. oz.	42	—	105	—	—	—	—	—	—	—	—	—	—	—	—	—
	Wines:																	
489	Dessert	3½ fl. oz.	100	—	137	—	—	—	—	—	8	8	—	—	0.01	0.02	0.2	—
490	Table	3½ fl. oz.	100	—	85	—	—	—	—	—	4	9	—	—	tr.	0.01	0.1	—
	Beverages, carbonated, sweetened:																	
491	Carbonated water (e.g. Tonic)	12 oz.	366	92	115	0	0	—	—	—	29	—	—	0	0	0	0	0
492	Cola type	12 oz.	369	90	145	0	0	—	—	—	37	—	—	0	0	0	0	0
493	Ginger ale	12 oz.	366	92	115	0	0	—	—	—	29	—	—	0	0	0	0	0
494	Bouillon cubes, approx. ½"	1 cube	4	4	5	1	tr.	—	—	—	tr.	—	—	—	—	—	—	—
495	Chocolate, bitter or baking	1 oz.	30	2	145	3	15	8	6	tr.	8	22	1.9	20	0.01	0.07	0.4	0
496	Chop suey, with meat or chicken	1 cup	155	—	180	16	10	—	—	—	8	36	2.9	360	0.17	0.23	3.0	20
497	Egg roll (pork)	2	146	—	479	7	42	5	13	18	18	28	1.5	240	0.14	0.14	1.5	10
	Gelatin:																	
498	Plain, dry powder in envelope	1 envelope	7	13	25	6	tr.	—	—	—	0	—	—	—	—	—	—	—
499	Dessert powder, 3 oz. pkg.	1 pkg.	85	2	315	8	0	—	—	—	75	—	—	—	—	—	—	—
500	Gelatin dessert, prepared with water	½ cup	120	84	80	2	0	—	—	—	19	—	—	—	—	—	—	—
501	Popsicle, 3 fl. oz. size	1 popsicle	95	80	70	1	tr.	—	—	—	17	tr.	tr.	0	tr.	tr.	tr.	—
	Soups:																	
	Canned, condensed, ready-to-serve:																	
	Prepared with an equal volume of milk:																	
502	Cream of chicken	1 cup	245	85	180	7	10	3	3	3	15	172	0.5	610	0.05	0.27	0.7	2
503	Cream of mushroom	1 cup	245	83	215	7	14	4	4	5	16	191	0.5	250	0.05	0.34	0.7	1
504	Tomato	1 cup	250	84	175	7	7	3	2	1	23	168	0.8	1200	0.10	0.25	1.3	15
	Prepared with an equal volume of water:																	
505	Bean with pork	1 cup	250	84	170	8	6	1	2	2	22	63	2.3	650	0.13	0.08	1.0	3
506	Beef broth, bouillon consomme	1 cup	240	96	30	5	0	—	—	—	3	tr.	0.5	tr.	tr.	0.02	1.2	—
507	Beef noodle	1 cup	240	93	70	4	3	1	1	1	7	7	1.0	50	0.05	0.07	1.0	tr.
508	Clam chowder, Manhattan type (with tomatoes, without milk)	1 cup	245	92	80	2	3	—	—	—	12	34	1.0	880	0.02	0.02	1.0	—

No.	Food	Measure	Weight	Moisture	Food Energy	Protein	Fat	Fatty Acids: Saturated (Total)	Fatty Acids: Unsaturated Oleic	Fatty Acids: Unsaturated Lin-Oleic	Carbohydrate	Calcium	Iron	Vitamin A Value	Thiamine	Riboflavin	Niacin	Ascorbic Acid
			g.	%	Cal	g.	g.	g.	g.	g.	g.	mg.	mg.	I.U.	mg.	mg.	mg.	mg.
	MISCELLANEOUS ITEMS (Continued)																	
509	Cream of chicken	1 cup	240	92	95	3	6	1	2	3	8	24	0.5	410	0.02	0.05	0.5	tr.
510	Cream of mushroom	1 cup	240	90	135	2	10	1	3	5	10	41	0.5	70	0.02	0.12	0.7	tr.
511	Minestrone	1 cup	245	90	105	5	3	—	—	—	14	37	1.0	2350	0.07	0.05	1.0	—
512	Split pea	1 cup	245	85	145	9	3	1	2	tr.	21	29	1.5	440	0.25	0.15	1.5	1
513	Tomato	1 cup	245	90	90	2	3	tr.	1	1	16	15	0.7	1000	0.05	0.05	1.2	12
514	Vegetable beef	1 cup	245	92	80	5	2	—	—	—	10	12	0.7	2700	0.05	0.05	1.0	—
515	Vegetarian	1 cup	245	92	80	2	2	—	—	—	13	20	1.0	2940	0.05	0.05	1.0	—
	Dehydrated, dry form:																	
516	Chicken noodle (2-oz. package)	1 pkg.	57	6	220	8	6	2	3	1	33	34	1.4	190	0.30	0.15	2.4	3
517	Onion mix (1½-oz. package)	1 pkg.	43	3	150	6	5	1	2	1	23	42	0.6	30	0.05	0.03	0.3	6
518	Tomato vegetable with noodles (2½-oz. pkg.)	1 pkg.	71	4	245	6	6	2	3	1	45	33	1.4	1700	0.21	0.13	1.8	18
	Snack Foods:																	
519	Puffs, cheese flavoured, etc.	1 cup	28	—	160	2	10	—	—	—	16	—	—	—	—	—	—	—
520	Chips, shapes, etc. (corn)	1—1½ cup	28	—	160	2	10	—	—	—	16	—	—	—	—	—	—	—
521	White Sauce, medium	1 cup	250	73	405	10	31	16	10	1	22	288	0.5	1150	0.10	0.43	0.5	2
	Yeast:																	

This bodyshape book should be able to help you in many ways. Good habits, once formed, have a way of snowballing. Just think what changes could take place in your life if you developed a new bodyshape. . .the possibilities are endless.

With strict adherence to this advice you should be able to work wonders. Never allow your body to lose its dynamic appeal. The price of staying in condition is, like freedom, eternal vigilance. But it can be fun.

To my mind, the most important ingredient in improving bodyshape is motivation. If you really want to look attractive again, then keep that thought ever-present in your mind. Make the decision now. Never give up.

As I see it, we have two choices in life:

1. We can take the joys of life as they present themselves. We can smoke heavily. We can drink all the booze that takes our fancy. We can eat candies, cookies, pies, pastas and spend our spare time gaping at the TV for amusement.

2. Or alternatively we could choose to take steps to safeguard our health by not smoking or drinking excessively. We could eat nutritious non-synthetic and non-fattening foods.* Follow a healthy regime of regular exercise and sensible living habits. It is my belief that the latter choice is the correct one. Make your decision now.

May good luck follow you through life!

*Actually, all foods are fattening in that they contain calories. However, a person who has a snack of tomatoes and cheese instead of apple pie and cream is going to end up less fat as the years go by.

Beautiful Vera Christensen of Winter Haven, Florida, has been a weight trainer all her life. She instructs, writes about and photographs lady bodybuilders from all over North America. Her figure is considered to be as near perfect as is possible, showing strong curvacious form, vigor, health, inner and outer beauty.